**Iñaki Ábalos
Absolute Beginners**

PARK BOOKS

Contents

7–11 Prologue

13–18 Somatic-Grotesque

21–53 Architecture for the Search for Knowledge

55–91 A Conversation with Andrés de Vandelvira

93–131 A Monstrous Encounter Between Transcendentalism and Positivism

133–154 Robert Smithson: The Picturesque Entropologist

157–189 Three Delirious Skyscrapers

191–221 Dualisms

223–225 Photo Credits

226 Imprint

"The past is an animal that is always alive"
Alberto Conejero, playwright and poet

Prologue

Absolute Beginners is an essay on the forms of innovation in architecture. Built with diverse materials elaborated during the twenty years since the publication of *The Good Life*, it is not and does not pretend to be a sequel, but it maintains a similar interest to that book by examining questions centered on how and why architectural creation—at least the kind that arouses the greatest cultural interest—is strongly linked to philosophical thought, especially to the essay and the aphorism, and, particularly in the case of this new book, by attempting to understand why innovation—as happens in philosophy—is indissolubly linked to a reflection on the past; to the emergence of new ways of appropriating old problems.

A considerable span of time has elapsed between writing *The Good Life* and this volume, which gathers together a diverse range of texts. Some were necessitated by the system of academic promotion used by the polytechnical schools, which demands that research be submitted to contests in order to obtain academic positions; some were the result of invitations to different forums or linked with curation work; while others were produced for sheer pleasure, combined with personal need. All in all, I have produced a collection of essays that at each moment responded more or less fortuitously to the intersection of the need to formally meet the institutional thematic framework and the need to surrender to my interests and obsessions. Thus, the content of *Absolute Beginners* is composed of originally heterogeneous materials: research required to receive a professorship at the ETSAM in Madrid (which took the form of an analysis of the parallels between Frederick L. Olmsted and Le Corbusier); followed by research required to obtain the position of Chair of the Department of Architecture at Harvard, and years later to bid farewell to that position with the traditional Walter Gropius Lecture (a great honor for which I focused on the architectural implications of Nietzsche's aphorism "Architecture for the Search for Knowledge"). These "official" works are interwoven with texts composed for pure enjoyment, like the impossible interview with Andrés de Vandelvira, a surreal whim to which I devoted myself from time to time over the course of a decade; journalistic articles like "Somatic-Grotesque," initially written for *Babelia* (a weekly cultural supplement in *El País*; or opening and closing remarks at symposia organized together with a select group of professors that I have collated here as an essay on the modernity of monstrous beauty under the title "Dualisms."

I have also included texts linked to exhibitions I have curated, and for whose catalogs I produced essays, as I did enthusiastically for the one held at the Círculo de Bellas Artes in Madrid exhibiting for the first time all the originals of the wonderful book *Alpine Architecture* by Bruno Taut. Or the essay and project developed for the exhibition celebrating 100 years of Madrid's Gran Vía, held in the Telefónica building (located at the epicenter of Gran Vía), to which I invited a group of (then) young colleagues who are all superb and renowned architects today. And, more recently, the presentation I put together for the seventeenth edition of the Venice Biennale under the title "Atemporal Communal Palaces," which resulted from several courses I gave at both the ETSAM and the GSD that, after being revised and expanded with the help of research associates from both centers (José de Andrés Moncayo, Sofía Blanco Santos, and Armida Fernández), have given rise to an essay that is largely a tribute to the intellectual freedom of Roland Barthes and his course How to Live Together, which he held in 1972 at the Collège de France at the invitation of Michel Foucault, and which is also a great inspiration in my approach to writing and design.

All these works and their different formats have been brought together in seven revised chapters and thoroughly reworked, to the point where it can be said that this book is in itself a single essay that expands on and completes many of the original themes of *The Good Life*. It is an essay that questions the role of the past in what could be called the vast legacy of disruptive innovation that from the High Middle Ages to the present day has constituted the core that sustains the figure of the architect and their work as it is understood, at least up to the present day, by most in urban and academic culture.

This book is not meant to be a compilation of heterogeneous materials but a single essay constructed with effort and passion from the materials I just listed, made for the pure pleasure of composing a new and complex work, understanding the starting documents as necessary fragments, while remaining open to adjustments, changes, and bridges between them, including where I thought it was convenient to use reiterations or "refrains," composing all of this with a

technique that you might call musical. This method of
working was largely inspired by how the recording studios
in the late sixties came to be understood as just another
musician, a key player in the process of organizing the
heterogeneous materials and constructing a cohesive
composition from them: this happened with the Beatles and
the Beach Boys, of course, who locked themselves up
in the studios; and more recently with musicians like Brian
Eno, David Bowie, or David Byrne, who adapted this new
technique to the universe of digital sound; and, coinciding
with musical developments and almost on a par with them
in terms of contemporary influence, the great sonic outburst
that emerged from Jamaican Dancehall.

The book is thus a defense of the interest in studying how—
certainly over the arc of the modern era but also at
other moments—innovation arises from rethinking the past
through new technical and ideological prisms that are
almost always different from those applied in the past.
And in this sense, it is a deliberate wager to abandon the
extremely banal but widespread ideas about program
and place defended by functionalism and contextualism,
a wager that contains an unabashedly radical affirmation:
that a good idea in architecture is independent of time,
context, scale, and function, and is therefore open to multiple,
unprecedented explorations. The inverse formulation of
this statement is also true: it is always interesting to
implement good architectural ideas, whatever their scale,
context, program, or period.

Absolute Beginners is particularly interested in the way
in which the idea of Picturesque beauty defined by Uvedale
Price at the end of the eighteenth century modified the
classical ideal by introducing an aesthetic based on an
empiricist vision of nature, which had a decisive influence on
the creativity of key figures of modernity such as Frederick
Law Olmsted and later Le Corbusier—who was a living
influence on a wide range of authors throughout the arc of
modernity—and which in the mid-twentieth century provided
the basis for Robert Smithson's sculptural postulations
and with him, many of the practices now commonplace in
contemporary art. The book also focuses on the great
discovery made by the first Picturesque authors of the need for
certain degrees of ugliness in order to achieve a new
notion of beauty, a "Frankenstein effect" that crosses the
entire arc of modernity in architecture, literature, film, and

the visual arts. Furthermore, it goes back to medieval architecture, to the monastic interpretation of the Romanesque and the Gothic, and its obsessive construction of monumental typologies devoted to facilitating a new and fruitful spiritual contemplative life, ideas that with the conquering of the seas and contact with other peoples and cultures gave rise to cross-fertilizations and hybridizations of a typological, formal, and material nature, with admirable solutions of integration and adaptation that became particularly prevalent in Latin America. In short, the book narrates and speculates on the difficulties and passionate negotiations between the past and innovation that the best creators accepted as necessary conditions of achieving new forms of beauty.

Absolute Beginners ultimately demands—especially from the younger generations—that we recognize the need to look for solutions in the remote past, in the accumulated knowledge of the discipline, and in the examples set by the great creators capable of seeing the future in the past, and of seeing it sometimes with the extraordinary innocence of absolute beginners.

I would like to thank Thomas Kramer for his interest in and commitment to making this book since we produced the English edition of *The Good Life* together for Park Books, and also for the freedom and time he has given me to do so, which has been both rewarding and enjoyable.

I would also like to thank José de Andrés Moncayo and Sofía Blanco Santos for the invaluable support their collaboration has provided me, bringing order to the initial chaos, helping me to weave together and give continuity to texts that were initially unconnected and to test their content in the Master's in Advanced Architectural Projects in 2019/2020, making the first mock-up of the book and helping to review the final selection. This book would not have been possible without their help and that of Renata Sentkiewicz, who has filled in for me, allowing me the time and concentration I needed, so that the process of writing the book could be the way I desired, making the experience of writing and rewriting it a source of pleasure, knowledge, and joy.

Iñaki Ábalos

Somatic-Grotesque

View of the grotto in the Parc des Buttes-Chaumont, Jean-Charles Alphand. Paris, 1867

The grotto is the ultimate architectural interior. Since its revival in the imagination of the English Picturesque empiricists of the eighteenth century, the grotto has continued to excite a fascination that has secretly run through modernity, always vying for supremacy with the idea of exteriority, which here and there delights in taking flight and dominating from a panoptic viewpoint. In fact, the grotto represents the very core of architecture, the need for inner force, an obscure, atavistic center that refuses, opposes, and counters transparency, visibility, and lightness. This fascination triggers a generalized attraction that transcends professional debate. The cave was the first interior to be discovered by humankind and it continues to exert an influence that could be described as a primordial somatic drive. Jean-Charles Alphand's success in transforming the galleries of the mines of Buttes-Chaumont into the caves of Paris's first great Picturesque park brought the grotto out of its initially private setting—English country homes of the eighteenth and nineteenth centuries—and turned it into a new kind of public space. Its success was certainly the result of something more complex than just visual curiosity. In the grotto, in interiors, the human body inverts its conventional relation with the outside world and, from a technical viewpoint, transforms from an irradiated into a radiating body. Electromagnetic waves circulate in the opposite direction: rather than the sun, it is we who emit them, giving us the characteristic sensation of cold that is always greater than the thermometer registers; our body and our sensorium activate a dialogue with earthy matter, humidity, and geomorphologic darkness of an intensity that is unknown "out there." When Nietzsche said "We wish to see *ourselves* translated into stone and plants, we want to take walks *in ourselves*," he was simply expressing this need to counter perception with more primary impulses in order to achieve knowledge (see aphorism 270, "Architecture for the Search for Knowledge," in *The Gay Science*).[1]

Like other human beings, when architects reach maturity, they often feel the attraction of the grotto, the call made by the telluric abyss. I could cite many names and cases; for example, Hans Poelzig and The architects involved in Die Gläserne Kette (The Crystal Chain) exploited this Picturesque, Romantic vein from an Expressionist or nihilist perspective. Later, in Mexico, Juan O'Gorman followed a similar path to many others when he shifted radically from the Modernist

[1] Nietzsche, F. (1974). *The gay science*. Vintage Books.

lightness of his early house for Rivera and Kahlo to the interior excavated from lava stone of his own home in his mature years, as did Frederick Kiesler with his Endless House and César Manrique with his home in Lanzarote. For these architects, the cave represented liberation, preventing the construction of a world of distributive rationality, etiquette, and codified domestic rituals, because it is brought to us in its natural condition, as a pocket produced by telluric forces that are completely detached from the concept

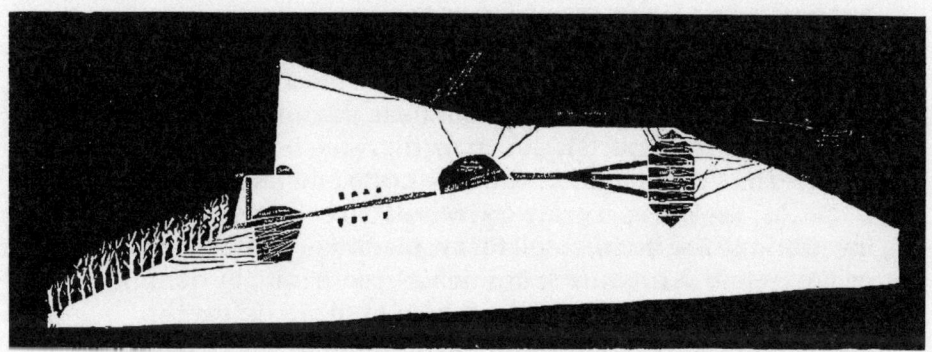

Basilique de La Sainte-Baume, Le Corbusier. France, 1948

of codified routines. The cave is a topological formation that is free of the imprint of culture and sees domestic ritual converted into banal artifice. The grotto guarantees a degree of impunity, facilitating an almost total invisibility where the self becomes a natural body, striking up an intimate dialogue with the other elements of nature with which it coexists: lava, the force of earth and fire, air, light, and humidity. The grotesque is the form that architects have repeatedly used to introduce—almost brutally—natural time into space, enabling them to deploy a fabulous world of images, of fantasies that rush instantly into our minds and make us see what we do not see, shifting from the three planes of architecture to the fourth dimension, to the unfolding of time and our passing presence within it. Le Corbusier perfectly illustrates this atavistic call, for which it is hard to find examples from his early years. Fascinated by lightness and the ability to fly, architects are first Icarus and later, often quite suddenly, they not only come back down to earth but also compulsively start to work with its interiority. Le Corbusier, fascinated in his youth by the power and the scale of the Machine Age, Taylorist methods, and the new industrial materials, embarked on his professional adventure by imagining objects that barely touched the ground, that were always light and elevated, always towering regally over the landscape, for the observation of which he invented ribbon windows, horizontal like the landscape they reflected. Initially, he merely drew undulating woods among his skyscrapers to reconcile the Machine Age and the Picturesque, but by the late 1920s his walks on the beach had led him to collect sensually shaped found objects such as stones, driftwood, bones, and shells that he termed "objects of poetic reaction" and which might have caught his eye due to their similarity to purist, Cubist forms. This hobby would soon lead to a fascination with concrete and its material qualities, as well as a growing interest in shadows—with the invention of the brise-soleil that replaced his pure glass prisms—and in organic forms, which were initially confined to the internal partition wall but later came to define the shape for entire buildings. But no sooner did he reach his sixties than Le Corbusier made the decisive step of addressing the mountain and a religious brief, a basilica in the Sainte-Baume (1948). He created a complex contrivance in the form of a great bridge that brought the faithful from the plains to the intermediate slopes of the rocky mass of the mountain of Sainte-Victoire and drew them into a great hollowed-out cave, reminiscent of the belly of Jonah's whale. This project marked a spectacular change in the way he addressed space, which would guide all of his mature work, effecting a complete turnaround in the direction taken by modernity, which to a large extent followed in his wake. Le Corbusier's masterwork of the period in Ronchamp—a constructed cave—cannot be construed without this initial project, nor can we understand much of what happened in architecture in the following decades without Ronchamp.

From here, we move forward in time and visit OMA's proposal for the Bibliothèque de France (1989), with a section that could be regarded as the seminal outline of contemporary architecture. There is no need to repeat its associations with the references described here; what is interesting in this section, conversely, is the new light it casts on interpreting both the cave and the high-rise construction, completely reversing the principles of exteriority that initially made the

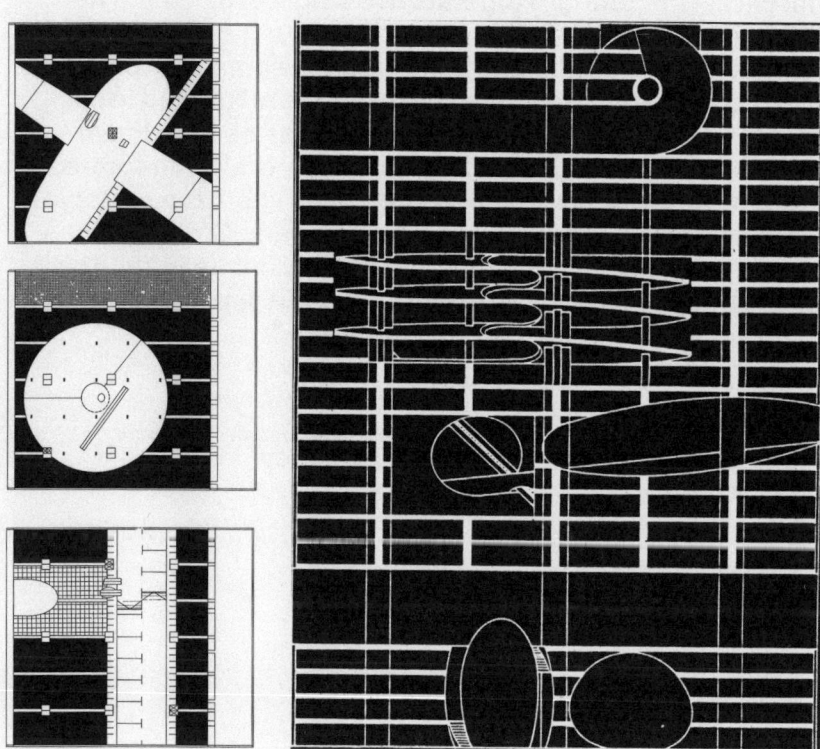

Plans and section for Très Grande Bibliothèque, OMA. Paris, 1989

skyscraper an apparently consolidated typology. The cubic mass of stored information that configures the volume of the section—basically an immense high-rise archive—forms within it an artificial environment. Here, a series of concatenated volumes that owe as much to the *promenade architecturale* as to the Picturesque grotto, excavate spaces for public uses, floating in the amniotic fluid of knowledge. All relations between nature and artifice are inverted, and both internal and external experience seem to explore the extent to which our somatic systems can adjust to a complete alteration of the physical environment. What was once a topology sunk into the ground—the grotto—rises, concealed now in a volume without attributes, pure shaped mass. That which the body experienced as an intensified dialogue with the natural environment is established now as a completely artificial setting. Forms which modernity separated into two opposite polarities—the skyscraper and the cave—are brought together in a single organism. The different somatic impulses—the vertigo of height and panoptic vision on the one hand, and the somatic experience and the activation of time on the other—are trapped in a grotesque formation that imposes itself as new, artificial nature. Here, the skyscraper-cave duality is also integrated into a more complex whole that could be seen as a prototype of a new kind of compact, atmospheric park. Grotto, skyscraper, and park are, then, one and the same thing. This "same thing" calls for the reinvention of our subjectivity in the construction of a new "experience."

Bibliography:
Nietzsche, F. (1974). *The gay science*. Vintage Books.

Architecture for the Search for Knowledge

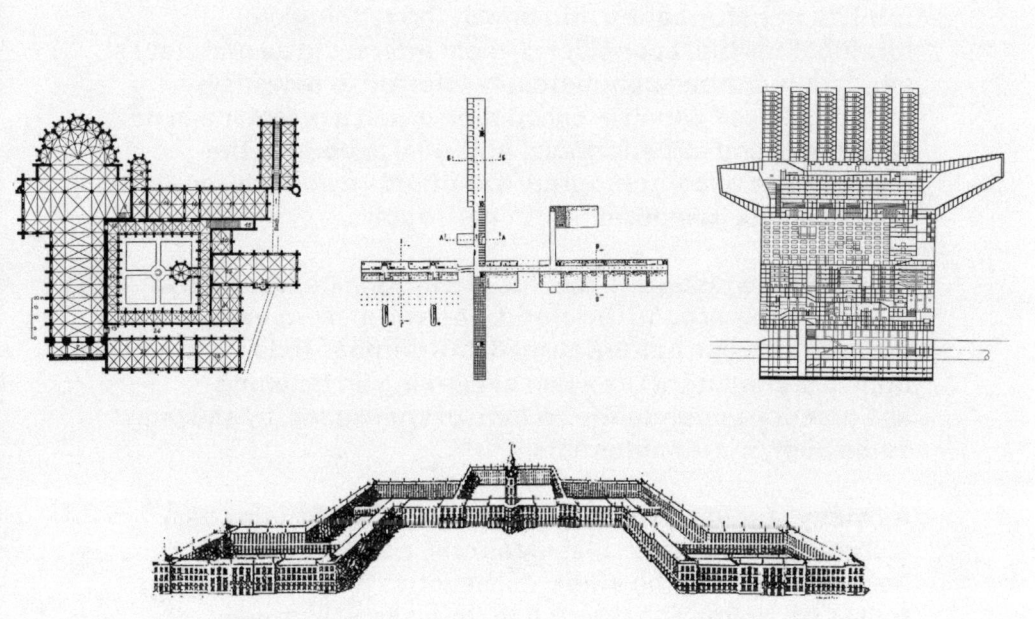

Monastery of Royaumont, 1228–1235
Communal House, Mikhail Barshch and Vladimir Vladimirov, 1929
Atlanpole, Hans Kollhoff, 1988
Phalanstère, Charles Fourier, 1822

Thank you all for being here tonight. To celebrate the occasion of this talk, I have chosen a subject on which I don't believe anybody can consider themselves an expert, a subject that is a central theme of academic activity and particularly of the GSD and its Department of Architecture: that of the relationship between education, research, and professional practice.

I will address this theme by way of a curious and almost forgotten architectural type, the medieval monastery, following its somewhat paradoxical evolution through time until its transformation into one of the typological formulations that I consider of most interest to an architect's education: the one commercially referred to nowadays as "mixed use," which in my opinion is just a prototype in its childhood, and has enormous potential to combat the dismal state of contemporary architecture and improve quality of life, transforming our metropolis.

Many of the students in this room will soon be teachers at other schools around the world, and will disseminate the GSD's design culture abroad. My purpose today is to give them a testimony of the value of working on teaching and practice understood as a form of knowledge, by showing some of my current interests.

As many studio instructors do, I use Option Studios as a laboratory where I can test ideas still in the process of becoming, giving the students an active role in identifying routes of exploration through their designs. Normally this experience is translated into exhibitions or into essays or articles which pose new questions and give birth to new studios, and so on. This year's Option Studio, "Subjects, Forms, and Performances of the Contemporary Hybrid," is testing protocols of design based in exploring the lineage of the contemporary mixed-use type in historic manifestations such as the medieval monastery and its successors in the socialist phalanstery or the communist *kommuna*. So this talk is in many ways its natural outcome. And why medieval monasteries? In recent years I have been asked frequently about my life in Cambridge, and I always had the same response: I live now like a monk, cloistered, my time divided up precisely between teaching, learning, practicing, writing, meeting, and writing emails. Every single day of the week.

It is kind of a banal response, as it is an experience that everyone has here, instructors and students alike. But its repetition got me interested in how monks actually lived in medieval times. What were their motivations, routines, and their forms of organization in architectural terms? What can I learn from them?

So it is only recently that I developed an interest in the typology of the Cistercian and Carthusian monastery, possibly because the immaculate type of the Gothic cathedral had—as it did for so many of us—obscured in my mind this other essential type of the medieval era. A type or typology that was seminal in producing much of what we know now, transmitting knowledge and paving the path for what we know as our universities.

I would like to show you some engravings and drawings representing the whole context of the monastery type, not only what we are used to seeing as their monumental core. These drawings representing the entire physical context of the monasteries impressed me because in them I understood that their eventual success and their productive culture were based in the land they owned. It allowed them not only to survive but also to interact with the surrounding villages through an intense economic exchange of goods, promoting the local markets and therefore the economy of the villages, and through increasingly large exchanges, giving way to a new form of territorial organization that opened the door to the Renaissance understandings of territory and culture.

In sum, they stopped looking to me like what we now call, in ecological terms, "closed systems." Because I discovered that in reality they operated as "open systems." The spatial mechanism is the creation of spheres of decreased privacy, revolving around the church and the cloister. This central sphere is followed by other spheres that begin with the domestic domain of the converts, who are not dedicated to the contemplative life but serve as a labor force for agriculture, farming, hydrology, forging (bronze, tiles, glass), and the like, which in turn border another sphere occupying significant areas of land, and surrounded by the final one: the forests that border the property, and that, being wild nature, provide the resources for generating heat. This system of spheres of privacy has remained since then the main organizational tool of architecture's various mixed-use types.

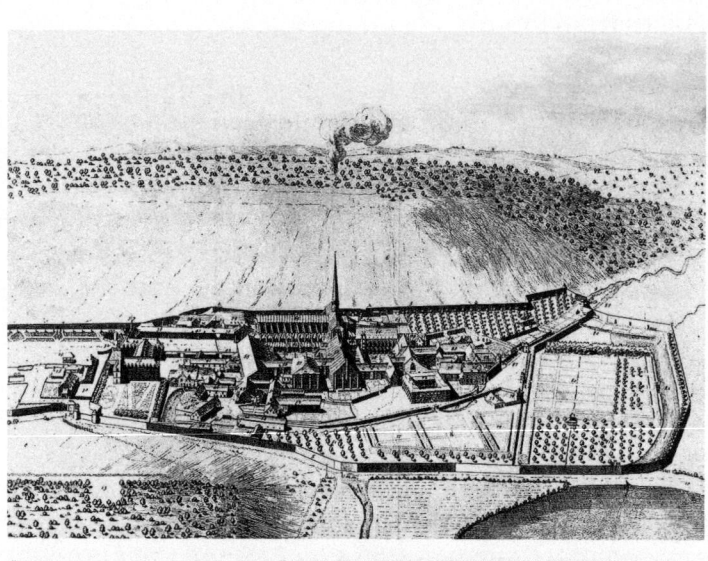
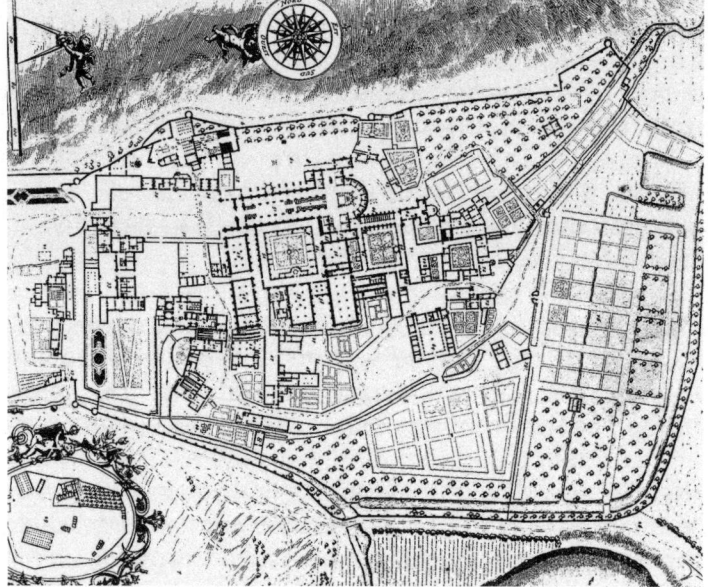

A view of Cluny Abbey ca. 1670, drawn by Louis Prévost
Plan of the Cistercian Monastery of Clairvaux. France, 1115. Drawing from 1708

In ecological terms, the monastery is the most successful mixed-use type of all. Both temporally and spatially. Temporally because of its endurance, surviving through to the present day; and spatially because of its successful spread throughout all the countries of Europe, making a unique contribution to the cultural and economic evolution of medieval villages.

For years I focused my attention on exploring the potential of the mixed-use type in Modernist and contemporary architecture, remaining somehow blind to its interesting ancestors. In one of my first articles, "Hybrids," I collected a series of complex structures that began to construct a genealogy of the mixed-use type.

This collection started with Sullivan's Romanesque Auditorium, before moving on to the impressive monolith of the John Hancock Center in Chicago, and continuing with some important unbuilt projects. After that, in *Tower and Office*—a book I published in English thanks to the generosity of Michael Hays's review of it, when he didn't know me at all—I studied in detail the evolution of the ideals of Modernist architects inspired by the Taylorist principles of the division of labor applied to the technical apparatus of the skyscraper: program, structure, façade, core, MEP, etc., with each part receiving a separate approach and treatment. The post war developments actually demonstrated that the reality was very much the opposite. The parts contributed to the whole, merging systems and programs and contradicting the spatial and organizational logics of the monofunctional skyscraper, making its design a new site where all the subsystems have to adapt, negotiate, and collaborate to subsist. These examples represent a moment in the long process that occurs in between an original experimental prototype and its typological consolidation, constructed by addressing the material culture of a given moment in time. A significant part of my research has been dedicated to explaining this prototype, the mixed-use type, as an embryo of a forthcoming metabolic entity that is potentially (highly) efficient in social, ecological, and thermodynamic terms, using my teaching and practice to experiment with new design protocols that resist the most obvious commercial clichés, confronting them with categories such as monstrous beauty, dualisms, or the thermal engine, which seek to open new paths for the evolution of the mixed-use type. Revising the article

26 Architecture for the Search for Knowledge

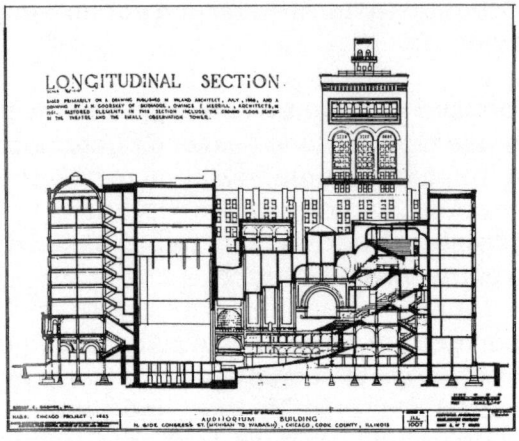

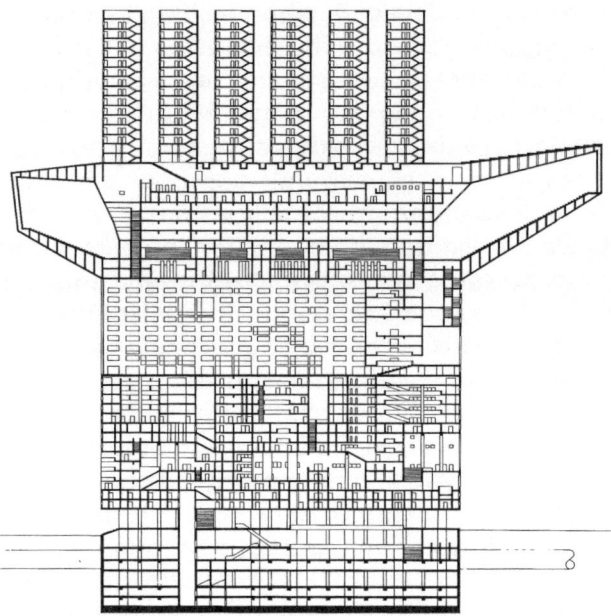

Auditorium Building, Louis Sullivan. Chicago, 1887–1889
Atlanpole, Hans Kollhoff. Nantes, 1988

"Hybrids" some twenty-five years later, I see that the
schemes that were less commercial and somehow more
visionary were the ones that captured my attention,
such as OMA's library design for Paris and its new formulation
of the tower that reversed its Modernist interior/exterior
relations, or the massive vertical orchestration of multiple
typologies—private and public—in Kollhoff's Atlanpole.
The first used intrusion as its main design technique, the
intrusion of an extended Picturesque version of Le Corbusier's

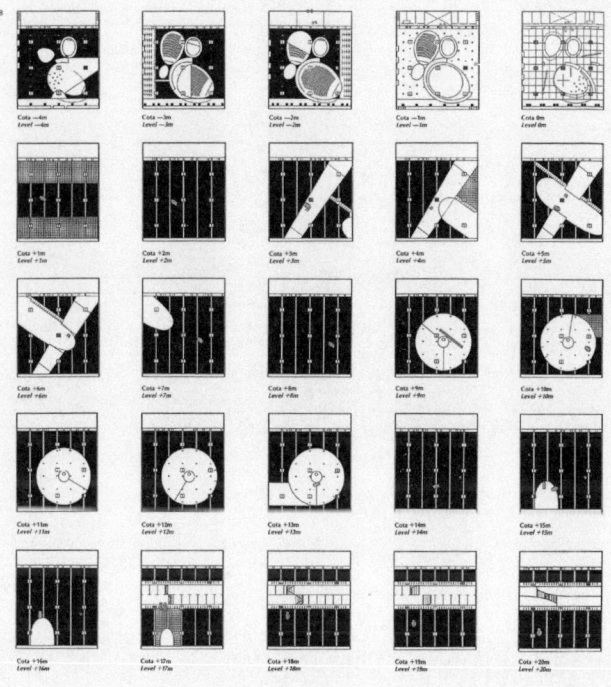

promenade; the second monumentalized the silhouette of
the mixed-use type as a massive sculpture. Just to mention a
few examples that to my mind resonate with the title I
borrowed from Nietzsche for this lecture, "Architecture for
the Search for Knowledge," a title that belongs to the
aphorism numbered 280 in his book *The Gay Science*, first
published in 1882. This is an aphorism I have quoted—not by
coincidence—in the three books that I consider most
relevant in my career: *Tower and Office*, *The Good Life*, and
Essays on Thermodynamics, Architecture and Beauty.
So let's take a look at this aphorism.

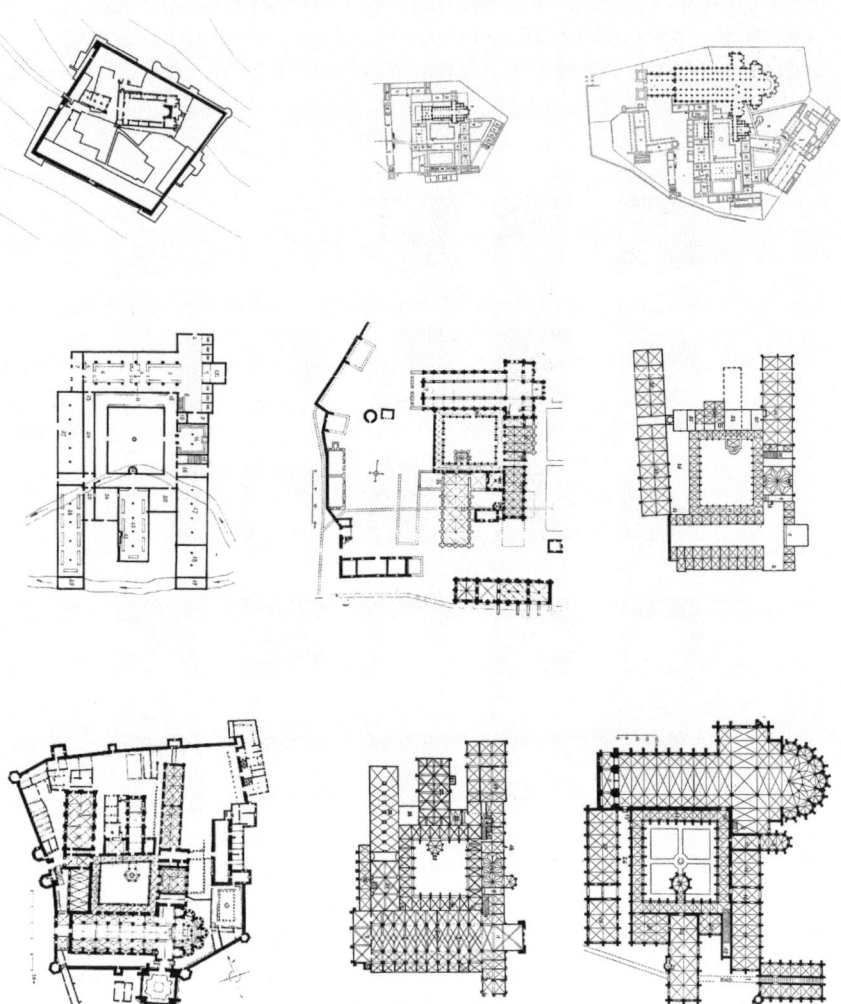

(From left to right and top to bottom) Monasteries of St. Catherine, Cluny I, Cluny III, ideal plan for a Cistercian monastery, Fontenay, Eberbach, Poblet, Maulbronn, Royaumont

Part 1: Monasteries

> One day, and probably soon, we need some recognition of what above all is lacking in our big cities: quiet and wide, expansive places for reflection. Places with long, high-ceilinged cloisters for bad or all too sunny weather where no shouting or noise of carriages can reach and where good manners would prohibit even priests from praying aloud—buildings and sites that would altogether give expression to the sublimity of thoughtfulness and of stepping aside. The time is past when the church possessed a monopoly on reflection, when the *vita contemplativa* always had to be first of all a *vita religiosa*; and everything built by the church gives expression to that idea. I do not see how we could remain content with such buildings even if they were stripped of their churchly purposes. The language spoken by these buildings is far too rhetorical and unfree, reminding us that they are houses of God and ostentatious monuments of some supramundane intercourse; we who are godless could not think *our thoughts* in such surroundings. We wish to see *ourselves* translated into stone and plants, we want to take walks *in ourselves* when we stroll around these buildings and gardens.[1]

This last phrase is an amazing architectural micro-manifesto whose beauty is almost impossible to resist; it persuades purely because of its beauty. Believe me or not, throughout the years that I quoted it, I was unaware of how much Nietzsche was thinking about a specific architectural type. I thought it was a generic, Gothic and Picturesque dream. Only now that I have grown interested in monasteries as a typology can I see that he writes the whole paragraph with a specific monastery in mind. Before I analyze this text in detail, though, let me invite you to gain an impression of the atmosphere of the monasteries, in their main spaces and rooms, by taking a stroll around their stones and gardens through a selection of images from different monasteries, chosen to give you a broad sense of their differences.

---

[1] Nietzsche, F. (1974). *The gay science*. Vintage Books.

There is the chapter house, the place where monks and abbot read and comment upon the monastic rule, the rule that governs their life and is organized in chapters. The cloister, where they wander around, alone and in silence, or all together in a procession, the squaring of the cloister being a representation of divine perfection in its length, height, width, and depth. The fountain, a very symbolic element providing life and purity. The refectory, where the monks all gather together, but in silence or to read. The library, where they study or copy books. The dormitory where everybody sleeps, with the exception of the abbot. The church, where they sing the psalms and celebrate divinity. The choir, the place reserved for the monks to celebrate the mass. The kitchen, the thermodynamic center of the monastery, close to the refectory and the calefactory, which is warmed and used as a sitting room, especially for sick and elderly monks. And the gardens, where they enjoy their limited spare time.

Nietzsche's aphorisms can be read just as we view these images: as poetry. They are poetry and they are philosophy in its most rhetorical state, not subject to any of the predicaments of formal logical protocols.

Aphorisms are essays or micro-essays that project ideas in their most intuitive state, solely searching for rhetorical persuasion. This is something that brings them close to the act of designing, which also consists in projecting ideas, crystallized into forms, seeking to persuade of their appropriateness and importance. To associate the architectural project to the essay brings together the spheres of philosophy and architecture, of space and time, as the beam and underside of knowledge. It is therefore not surprising that philosophy uses architectural metaphors and that architecture needs philosophical ideas. More importantly, we can see aphorisms as synthetic written forms that crystallize ideas, reactions, readings, or discussions that remain vague and disperse, floating without focus until the moment they find a synthetic presentation and become articulated as a whole. Only after this form takes shape as a provocation can a potential path of research be developed.

I am talking about the analogy between aphorisms and projects because in my mind there is a central idea: as happens with aphorisms, projects come first. They act on us as agents of revelation; there is not a neat cause-effect relationship between research and project. If anything, it is the other way around. The project comes to us in all its complexity at a given moment, suddenly, and imposes its logic on all previous information, which has just been waiting for this moment, as if warming up. It is only once the project is in front of us that we can identify a research topic that needs to be articulated.

Perhaps I am being too radical and projects don't come before everything else all on their own. They appear in front of us as if they preceded everything else due to their presentation as a synthesis, as facts. But we have to admit that they actualize disordered ideas, conversations, images, memories, readings; all of them suddenly crystallized in a completely new format. So new that it connects all that was informal and chaotic, nonsensical, into precisely the opposite: pure order and form. And this idea has consequences for the way we might conceive the respective roles and moments of design and research.

Getting back to Nietzsche, he begins his aphorism with two obvious rhetorical devices. A future that he visualizes, "*One day, and probably soon,*" and an us, a "*we*" that presupposes and wishes to involve the reader, anticipating an audience. If we accept becoming part of his audience, we will believe that architecture produces knowledge, or that it *should* produce it. And we will want to know what is lacking in our big cities. It is in these questions that we are captured.

Nietzsche continues by saying that "The time is past when the church possessed a monopoly on reflection, when the *vita contemplativa* always had to be first of all a *vita religiosa*" and we, being impious/godless, could not have access to the knowledge in its constructions. "We wish to see *ourselves* translated into stone and plants, we want to take walks *in ourselves* when we stroll around these buildings and gardens." And that is where Nietzsche takes us. To an affirmation that we can all understand, but which makes a countermodel of the original model of the monastery. The paradox behind Nietzsche's aphorism is that the architectural image is used not as a model, but as a countermodel. What we don't want, but for which we have no alternative model. We can't talk about it in another language or through other forms, since they don't exist. Nevertheless we desire them, we need them. We want the monastery and we don't want it.

Chapter House, Cathedral of Wells. England, 1310
Cloister in the Benedictine Monastery of Santo Domingo de Silos. Spain, 954
Refectory in the Cistercian Monastery of Santa Maria de la Huerta. Spain, 1150
Library in the Carthusian Monastery of Montalegre. Spain, 1415
Cloister in the Carthusian Monastery of San Lorenzo di Padula. Italy, 1306
Dormitory in the Cistercian Monastery of Eberbach. Germany, 1136
Church of the Cistercian Monastery of Fontenay. France, 1118

Chapter House, Cathedral of York. England, 1342
Fountain in the Cistercian Monastery of Poblet. Spain, 1151
Church of the Cistercian Monastery of Fontenay. France, 1118
Church of the Benedictine Monastery of St. Etienne. France, 1136
Choir in the Cathedral of the Benedictine Abbey of Gloucester. England, 1089–1499
Kitchen of the Carthusian Monastery of S. Lorenzo di Padula. Italy, 1306

So perhaps it is the moment to ask ourselves how these architectures for the search for a divine knowledge were organized. Originally, they took the form of refuges in which individuals could isolate themselves completely from the world, like hermits in grottoes, and evolved very

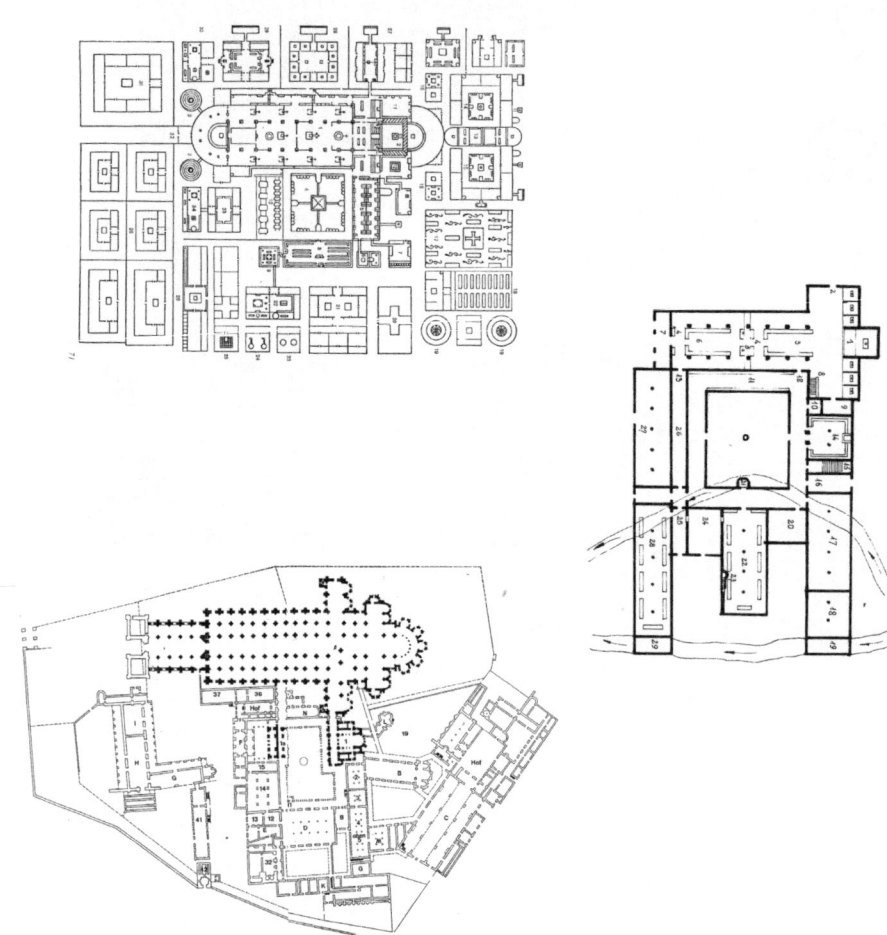

Plan of the Benedictine Monastery of Saint Gall, AD 820. Drawing by Haito, Abbot of Reichenau and Bishop of Basel
Ideal plan of a Cistercian Monastery
Benedictine Monastery of Cluny III., France, AD 1088

slowly into cenobitic organizations in forms that took centuries to consolidate. A bit of etymology about these words—monastery derives from *monazein* (live alone), while cenobite traces back to *kionos* (common) and *bios* (life)—shows the dual character of the monastery, living alone but having at the same time a common life. We see in the accompanying figures some of these moments when the monasteries retired to the desert, and the cloister then taking form later as an essential representation of the cenobitic life. A well-known moment in this evolution came in the year 820 with the Plan of Saint Gall. A plan that was drawn by Haito, Abbot of Reichenau and Bishop of Basel. Basel, the very place where Nietzsche had lived.

This is the earliest architectural plan that is known to us in Europe. It was the plan for the organization of an ideal monastery, removed from the world and self-sufficient. In it, we should point out the squared cloister attached to the church that organizes an interior for monastic life beside the church, normally in its southern orientation, taking advantage of the warmth of the sun for the daily life of the monks.

Without going into the controversies surrounding this document, it is both a diagram that divides up the programs, an inventory of the parts that allow the monastery to survive in its relative cenobitic isolation (although Saint Gall was an important pilgrimage site and a center of political power), and an initial approximation of a topological or relational scheme in which the location and contiguity of the different programs responds to an efficient organization on a flat and abstract site, governed only by the necessary east-west orientation of the church and the cloister, which as the core of monastery life received a more precise architectural definition.

The evolution of the prototype defined by this plan developed quickly between the eleventh and twelfth centuries, alongside the Benedictine Orders of Cluny and later the Cistercians of Saint Bernard.

Throughout these centuries, the overall form and material system of the monastery was perfected through the elaboration of a limited number of rooms arranged around the cloister (the chapter room, the refectory, the kitchen, the dormitories, the latrines, the church, etc.), complemented by the way the position of each constructive component and each different room becomes fixed in the cloister and the need for natural resources such as water. The architectural type of the Cistercian monastery is, in fact, the result of Saint Bernard's instruction to build near a river, which explains the position of the refectory and the kitchen.

Cistercian Monastery of Thoronet. France, 1176

Water is important for different purposes, so it is channeled and organized in two parallel waterways. One for drinking and cleaning, which serves as the source for the fountain, a fundamental element in the cloister; and another one for the watermills and to remove the waste that runs through the latrines and the kitchen.

This evolution follows a process of adaptation to the life of the monks, looking for the highest formal abstraction as an expression of knowledge that corresponds to the abstraction of the spiritual life they pursued. This progression from a prototype to a typology receives its definitive form to a great extent through the strong decision to use just one material, stone, which at the time was used only for cathedrals, fortifications, and palaces.

Stone has its own stereotomic rules that govern the shape of each different element and room in systemic ways. The Cistercian monastery is a celebration of stereotomic beauty in contrast to the ornamental character of Cluny's monasteries. Some of them, such as the well-preserved Monastery of Thoronet in France, are real manifestos of the power of abstraction in architectural forms, an abstraction that gives its character to the Cistercian monasteries, which cease to be interested in the fantasies of natural figurations that we can find in the monasteries of Cluny.

I mention all this to underline that typologies are not just diagrams or ideas. On the way to becoming types instead of experimental prototypes there is a process of finding their materiality and tuning it in tectonic, stereotomic, and thermodynamic terms, a process that gives its consistency and successful replication to the type. Typologies are not abstract ideas: they are made of matter, are based in a material culture, and only succeed through a happy encounter of form, matter, and flow.

This consistent unity of the monastery and its infrastructure, surrounded by auxiliary constructions, crops, and forests, generates a self-sufficient entity whose intrinsic beauty comes from being at once simple and complex. A machine for living, if I may borrow the words of Le Corbusier; or more precisely, a metabolic machine in which a small group of monks live under a series of precise, even mechanical rules and codes.

But what was the appeal of this invention, such that even the knights of the upper classes renounced their sumptuous and violent lives, their wealth, their most instinctive pleasures, in order to donate their goods and fortunes and commit themselves to the monastic life, choosing isolation and poverty?

The answer lies in the promise of happiness that the contemplative life offered, identified at the time with the superiority of spiritual and religious life. And what is happiness in cenobitic life? To cite the architectural historian Christine Smith: "The greatest good, *summum bonum*, is union with God, partly experienced in this life and fully realized in eternal life. Monasticism is the quest for union with God through prayer, penance and separation from the world pursued by men or women sharing a communal life."[2]

This machine for living therefore stands as the typological materialization of the lifestyle of a new alternative subject in the medieval context—the monk—who, through his life and routines, devotes himself completely to the discipline of the rules of the order to which he professes his faith, whose dictates meticulously shape his daily schedules and activities, with each day identical to the next.

Every three hours he visits the church, starting at 2 am to sing the Psalms, the slow rhythm of choral singing—and we might say of their life—adjusted to the large resonance chamber that is the church, at odds with the obsession against resonance we see nowadays in our performing arts centers. Other activities in the monks' schedule are meditating and praying, normally while walking around the cloister. And reading sacred texts, or transcribing in the library the preserved Greek, Roman, Hebrew, or Arabic books, which supposes a profane dimension to the medieval and post-medieval organization of knowledge and pedagogy that is of the utmost interest.

This scheme, at once a protocol of life and of architecture, admits some variations. If Saint Benedict and Saint Bernard gave birth to the prototype of the Cistercian monastery, Saint Bruno gave birth to the Carthusian monastery at the same time, looking for a more radical way of structuring the

[2] Quote from a lecture given by Christine Smith on the history of the monastery typology as part of the course Subjects, Forms and Performances of the Contemporary Hybrid, taught by Iñaki Ábalos and Sofía Blanco Santos at Harvard Graduate School of Design in the fall of 2016.

vita religiosa, increasing in this cenobitic life the hermetic component by imposing total silence and maximum isolation upon the monks. This interesting alternative to the Cistercian prototype replaces the collective dormitory with individual lodges that have their own orchard in the form

Monks entering the church and a monk reading in the cloister

of a patio, all organized around a central garden space where the fountain is normally situated.

In summary: the new subject, the rule, and the type in their ecological context, function as a mechanism in pursuit of an idea of happiness. The new subject, the rule, and the type are one and the same thing, and the three of them are necessary at an organizational, economical, tectonic, and ecological level, and compose an architecture and a knowledge that contributed paradoxically to the creation of a new world at odds with that of the monastery.

All of this had almost disappeared by Nietzsche's time. Henry VIII dissolved the monasteries in England in the late 1530s, beginning a process that spread to the Lutheran countries throughout the sixteenth century, followed by the Catholic countries in the wake of the French revolution. We can say that this model was brought down by its own success. Not only for having given birth to a new secularized and educated class, but also because the monks eventually renounced their own principles of poverty and isolation, in some cases returning to the city where they attacked the power of the church and the prince or the king, depicting them all as one and the same thing.

But this model also generated another, sumptuous typological version, the monastery-palace. El Escorial stands out as the first example of this type, which soon spread to other monarchies throughout the sixteenth and seventeenth centuries. The layout of El Escorial comprises a complex program, rigidly subject to the rules of symmetry, with the palace connected to the church by its axis, the monastery-cloister and the rest of the spaces to the right, and the court rooms and other multiple activities organized into a school on the left.

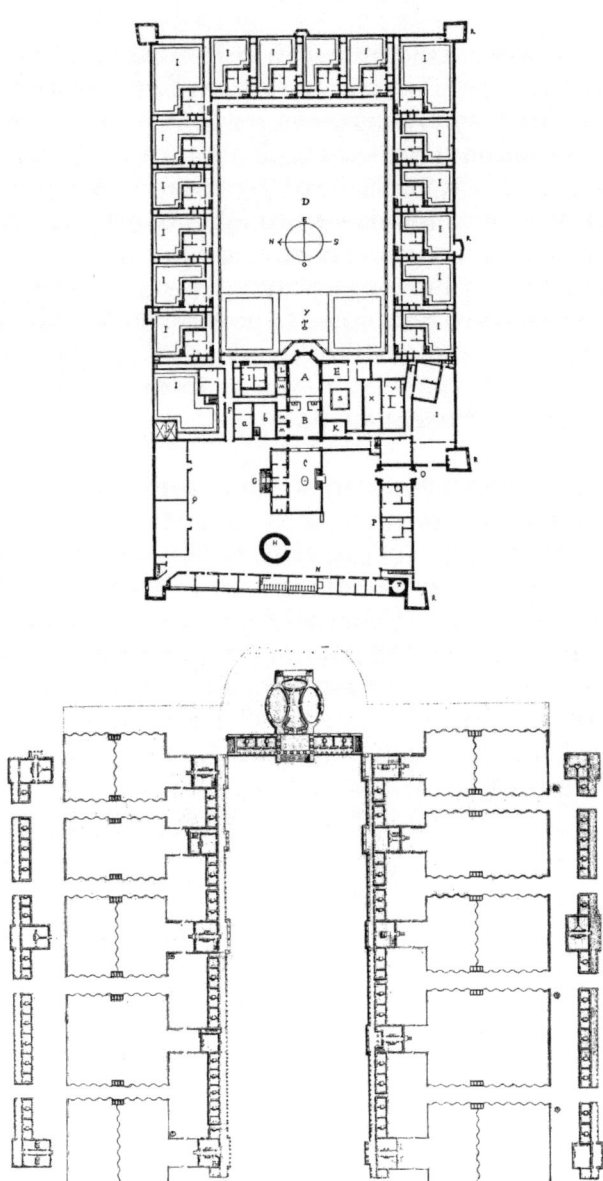

**Chartreuse de Clermont. France, 1219. Drawing by Viollet-le-Duc.
Virginia University Campus, Thomas Jefferson. Virginia, 1814**

Part II: Communal Palaces

I will not go into the sociopolitical implications of this typology. I will merely mention the indisputable interest of this new format of the monastery-palace as a typological invention, a monstrous hybrid, and a third version of the mixed-use type. It was also a typology that would lead to surprising new formulations in the first decades of the nineteenth century, when palaces and monasteries became points of reference for the revolutionary ideas of the "social condenser" and the campus university that the French (1789) and American (1775–1783) Revolutions propelled. Let's compare now these two successors to the monastery in this revolutionary period, by looking at the contributions of Thomas Jefferson and Charles Fourier.

Between 1819 and 1826, Thomas Jefferson, whose architectural skills were unquestionably superior to those of Fourier, designed and built the University of Virginia, a structure devoted to a secularized contemplative life in search of knowledge; and we all know just how successful this model was in spreading throughout the United States and the world. Jefferson proposed what is now a well-known distribution of pavilions around a central lawn, headed by a building that contains the most symbolic collective activities and leaving its other extremity open toward the natural landscape—though today it has unfortunately been closed off by new buildings.

It is impossible not to relate this typological scheme to the variation of the monastery type elaborated by the Carthusians from the eleventh century onward, in which each monk had his own house and orchard, and in which the entire composition is arranged around a central courtyard or garden, headed by the church, and further surrounded by a series of minor patios that allow for different functions and rituals.

I am not aware of whether Jefferson ever alluded to the typological similarity between the two models, or if he had visited any Carthusian monasteries during his time in France. What I am interested in is its formal and functional analogies. Formally, while Jefferson's campus maintains the typological scheme of the monastery, its Gothic vernacular disappears in favor of a Palladian, secularized one, then synonymous with the Enlightenment, a new civil culture. Functionally, Jefferson reproduced the isolation of the monks, with pavilions dedicated to specific disciplines and having a professor living on the upper floor, teaching his material in the lower rooms, while the students, as the new converts, were located on the perimeter, close to, but separated from, the inner ring.

It is no secret that American universities inherited the model of the medieval monastery, something that remains evident today in multiple aspects related to the regimented structure of campus life: from the language of academic hierarchies—provost, dean, chair, lecturer—all the way to the regalia that we wear during commencement ceremonies or the tight class schedules that meticulously organize our day-to-day. So none of these routines that I have been talking about are foreign to our daily lives, both of professors as monks and of students as converts, dedicated to a secularized form of knowledge.

In his excellent 1939 book *L'évolution pédagogique en France*, Emile Durkheim concludes by noting the notorious fact that among all the medieval institutions, it is the university that remains the closest to its original formulation. I only mention this to frame the intimate relationship this lecture has with all of us, who are somehow both its subjects and its objects.

The European idea of the phalanstery is firmly rooted in the ideas of utopian socialism in response to the impact of the modes of industrial production on the quality of life of the working class. And also against the lifestyle of a bourgeoisie that was completely indifferent to a situation that required urgent change. Like many other social critics, Charles Fourier saw this situation as an opportunity to propose a radically new subject as well as a new architectural prototype: the *Phalanstère*, whose name clearly alludes to its lineage, fusing phalanx, troop, or army, and monastery. For historical context, we are in the year 1822, contemporaneous with Jefferson's scheme, and six decades before *The Gay Science* was published.

The phalanstery represented an alternative to the prevailing modes of production, promoting the organization of the whole structure as a cooperative and alternative to the family unit, which was permitted but not needed or fostered (in fact, he proposed a familistery as a more moderate version).

For Fourier, just as for the Benedictine monks, happiness was at the core of his proposal. In Fourier's vision, it was an earthly happiness, a happiness for all both collective and individual, based on an improved organization of labor forces, freeing time for the pursuit of culture, but also for passions and other primary impulses, whose frustration was viewed as the root of all problems. For the first time in this lineage, this vision included the equal status of women (indeed the invention of the term "feminism" is often attributed to Fourier), and fueled libertarian anarchist theories, serving as inspiration for different attempts to materialize the phalanstery right through to the hippy communities of the sixties.

But we should not fool ourselves. The phalanstery materializes a way of life that is just as regulated and meticulously organized as the most structured systems of medieval, monastic regulations, from which it actually copies many of its guidelines, including somewhat surprisingly the organization into two social classes, just as in the medieval categories of the monks and the lay brethren, is divided according to their different social status.

Fourier proposes a community of around 1,600 inhabitants, so that its population and economy can be maintained long-term, housed in large linear structures organized around patios and galleries. The symmetry of the overall composition actually conceals a highly organized spatial zoning, with children occupying lateral wings where they are educated in the libertarian ideals, while the kitchen and the refectory are shared spaces, and the center of the composition is dedicated to art and knowledge, including a library and a theater.

The agricultural and industrial programs are located in front of the phalanstery, in a composition that could be seen as a new Plan of Saint Gall, although the phalanstery largely follows the aforementioned tendency to congregate monastic and palatial life in huge structures, with the king substituted here by individuals aspiring to a social form of happiness that melds work and passions. The phalanstery also embodies the utopia of a fully controlled environment, a utopia that is surely the expression of the contemporary development of hothouses, greenhouses, and stoves, announcing a new interest in comfort and climate that we may consider a kind of theological obsession: that of creating a paradise on Earth.

46 Architecture for the Search for Knowledge

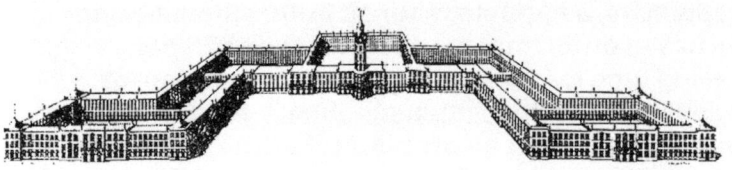

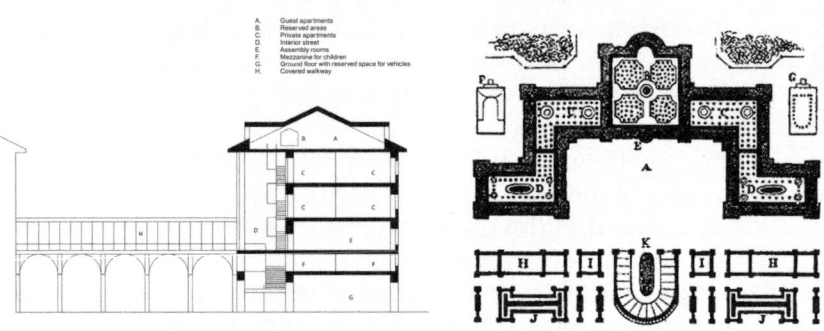

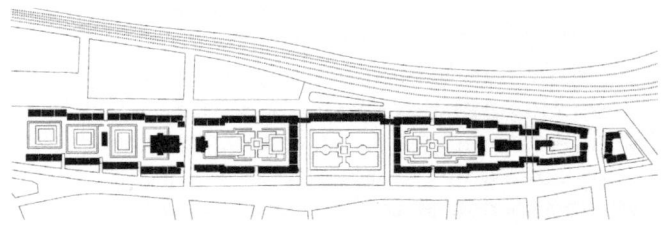

Phalanstère, Charles Fourier, 1822
Karl-Marx-Hof, Karl Ehn, 1927–1930

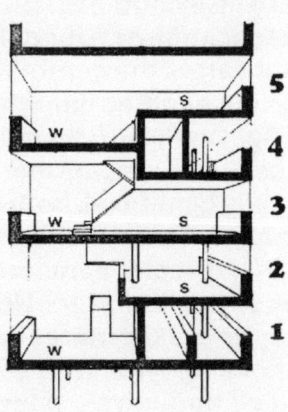
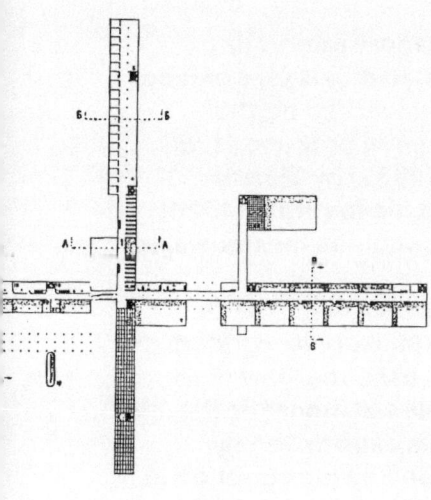
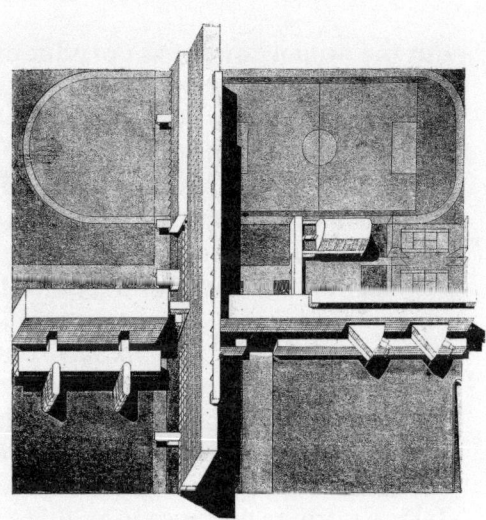
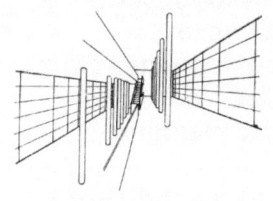

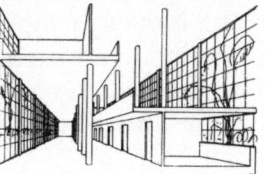

Narkomfin Building, Moisei Ginzburg and Ignaty Milinis, 1928–1932
Communal House, Mikhail Barshch and Vladimir Vladimirov, 1929

So at the beginning of the nineteenth century we see two different paths in the evolution of the typology of the monastery. Its replication as a model for the revolutionary universities emphasizes the centrality of knowledge and the isolation of cenobitic life, while the European social condenser focuses on the organization of alternative communities in search of a model that is productive, ecological, and psychologically beneficial, both for the individual and for the collective. This second trend finds its materialization in the social-democratic "Red Vienna," with the construction of the Karl-Marx-Hof in 1930, a grandiose structure measuring a kilometer in length, dedicated to massive social housing organized around a series of courtyards, divided through services such as maternity clinics, a health insurance office, laundries, and kindergartens, up to about twenty-five amenities that comprise an exuberant demonstration of the power of the working class, occasionally used more as a fortress than as a palace.

But the social condenser produced its more interesting examples after the Russian Revolution. Radical ideas of labor communes and an egalitarian society governed neither by the family unit nor by a divine order soon produced built examples like the Narkomfin Building (1932) by Moisei Ginzburg and Ignaty Milinis, or the Textile Institute (1929) by Ivan Nikolaev, in which the factory becomes the equivalent of the church in monastic typologies.

Not surprisingly, the rule of the communist social condenser, the *kommuna*, once more becomes an essential part of its typological definition. Similar to the rules of monastic life, life in the commune is chronometric, in this case driven by the fetishism of industrial production and by the adoption of Taylorist ideas of decomposing time into minimal units as small as two to three minutes. The new *kommuna* subject, who surrenders their family to the state and is supposedly fulfilled as an individual through their dedication to mechanized labor, will find a collective form of happiness in this world, but in a promised future that depends on their efficient work in the present and on state planning.

This idea found its own Plan of Saint Gall in the magnificent project for the Communal House (R.S.F.S.R.) designed by Mikhail Barshch and Vladimir Vladimirov in 1929. Its two linear buildings, curiously composed in a cross-shape, divide the 200 × 230 meter block into four open patios. The

intersection of these extremely thin volumes—the result
of the yearning for light and ventilation—divides the program
into a residential section running along the north-south
axis composed of individual cells measuring nine square
meters, a collective refectory, and other services. This thin
spine is intersected by the other east-west linear structure
that provides schools for the children on one side and
programs dedicated to the leisure time and reeducation of
the worker on the other.

The fetishism of the assembly line is not only present in the
extreme thinness of the slabs: it reaches its apogee in the
refectory, in which a mechanized system for the distribution
of plates, similar to the conveyor belts found in some
Japanese restaurants today, reinforces its linear organization.

The beauty of this stylized project and its faith in the rule/
type/material culture protocol adapted to the idea of a
communist form of happiness almost provides a caricature
of "modern times" (to borrow Charlie Chaplin's title),
symptomatic of the volatile condition of our time, and
in particular of the political agendas of the twentieth century,
with experiments that would have been of little or no
interest to Nietzsche, whose belief in the construction of a
new individual, the Übermensch, was far removed from a
socialized understanding of education and much closer to an
individualistic conception centered on the interior
struggles of a contemplative life.

A connection can be drawn here with the table I proposed in
Tower and Office that paid attention exclusively to the
other mode of the social condenser, the capitalist mixed-use
type, a product of the Cold War in many ways, ruled by
profits, consumerism, and technological exhibition, and
organized in vertical strata to minimize the repercussions on
land values. The substantial verticality of this type demanded
a new design technique based on organizing the section
instead of the floorplan as an adjustment of the gradients of
privacy between the flows of people in the street and
the demand for maximum isolation in the residential units
located at the top. To define the subject and the rules of this
iteration, we have to follow the flows of international
capital investments and of real estate data, painting a detailed
portrait of its Postmodernist character and its typical
inhabitant, no longer the Übermensch but the super-affluent
or super-rich, secluded in their golden towers in gigantic

cells fortified against any kind of otherness, as J. G. Ballard explained in his novel *High-Rise* (1975), now transformed into a curious film.

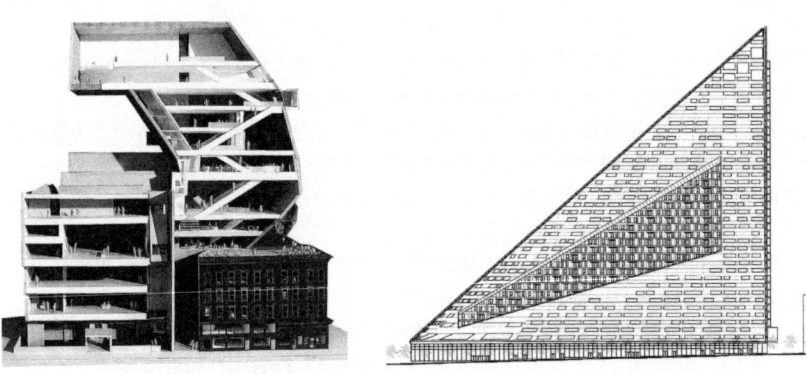

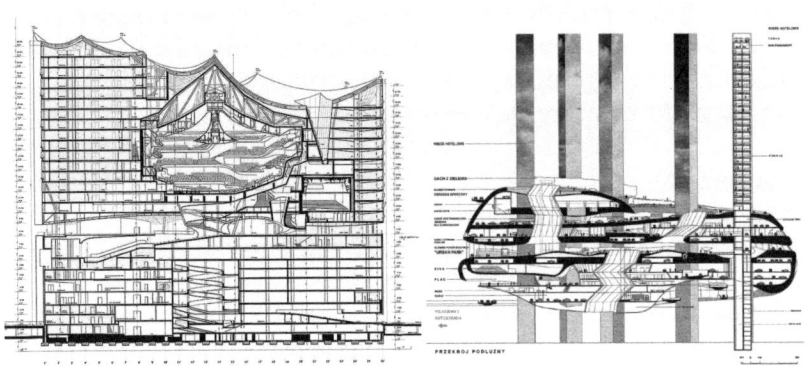

Whitney Museum extension, OMA. New York City, 2001
VIA57 West, BIG. New York City, 2014
Elbphilarmonie, Herzog & de Meuron. Hamburg, 2003–2016
Hotel & Leisure Center on the M-40 Highway, Ábalos+Sentkiewicz. Madrid, 1997

The most interesting built iteration of this idea can be found in the Waldorf Astoria in New York City, which was completed in 1931: the refined residential hotel as the capitalist alternative to the *kommuna*. But this is not the whole truth.

Today, a number of well-known architects—OMA, BIG, Herzog & de Meuron, and a number of others—have envisioned approaches that carry out interesting experiments with the potential inherent to this type, pursuing a conceptual reformulation of its social, urban, and methodological implications. In all cases we see the organizational emphasis transferred to the section.

Part III: Monsters

Our own office AS+ has contributed to this research and is dealing now with works that explore new urban and material complexes, presented very recently in this room in the context of the Heliomorphisms conference—so I am not repeating myself tonight.

As a professor at the GSD I have proposed protocols to the students that speculate with the vertical mixed-use type, applying design techniques that introduce basic thermodynamic principles, splitting the design process in two.

In the first phase, the organization of the projects focuses exclusively on conceiving them as thermal engines, using program as a combination of heat sources and sinks, and working with the equation form/matter/flow to manage climate, material, and sociocultural specificities. This moment produces what we call *monsters*, which are essentially aphoristic, to use the language of this lecture: provocations that help us to forget clichés and open the door to a second phase with the focus transferred to the students, who need to identify individual research projects to critically confront the inconsistencies, redundancies, and excesses of the first phase.

So to close this lecture: Where are we in this tale about the long lineage of the medieval monasteries conducted by Nietzsche as our master of ceremonies? What do we know? Honestly, it is very difficult to say, and first and foremost, it is very difficult to use the rhetorical "we" to respond to this question.

Although this is not a historical or political lecture, I am interested in the ideological differences and the methodological similarities of the mixed-use lineage. They all appear as countermodels of their predecessors. The monastery, the phalanstery, the campus, the *kommuna,* or the capitalist mixed-use type all reverse the main purposes of the one that precedes them, but contain similar outcomes and methods that reveal a trend. Nietzsche was right: we can learn from them if we understand them as countermodels. I see beauty in the search for knowledge in all of them. They are about innovation, type, and prototype; new ways of living, new forms of material culture, technology, knowledge, and they produce drawings, lots of beautiful drawings. But I do not see their beauty as something I or we can feel comfortable with.

It is here that I conclude my lecture without offering any neat conclusions, leaving them as a choice for each of you to deliberate, with a deep gratitude for having let me serve as the Chair of the Department of Architecture for these past years and for still being tied to a school that is faithful to the university principles of a dedication to knowledge and respect for the individuality and diversity of each one of us, teachers and students, monks and converts.

The text "Architecture for the Search for Knowledge" is a transcription of the Walter Gropius Lecture, presented by Iñaki Ábalos on November 29, 2016. The Water Gropius Lecture is the traditional lecture presented by the departing Chairs of the Department of Architecture of Harvard Graduate School of Design.

Bibliography:
Ábalos, I. & Herreros, J. (2003). *Tower and office: From modernist theory to contemporary practice.* Cambridge, MA: MIT Press.
Ábalos, I. & Ibañez, D. (2012). *Thermodynamics applied to highrise and mixed use prototypes.* Harvard Graduate School of Design.
Agamben, G. & Kotsko, A. (2013). *The highest poverty: Monastic rules and form-of-life.* Stanford University Press.
Ballard, J. G. (2012). *High-rise.* Liveright Pub.
Braunfels, W. (1993). *Monasteries of Western Europe: The architecture of the orders.* New York: Thames and Hudson.
Clifton-Taylor, A. (1967). *The cathedrals of England* (World of art library: Architecture). London: Thames & Hudson.
Conant, K. (1968). *Cluny: Les églises et la maison du chef d'ordre.* Cambridge, MA: Mediaeval Academy of America.
Durkheim E., & Halbwachs, M. (1938). *L'évolution pédagogique en France.* F. Alcan.
Eschapasse, M. (1963). *L'architecture bénédictine en Europe* (Architectures, no. 1). Paris: Éditions des Deux-Mondes.
Koolhaas, R. (1994). *Delirious New York: A retroactive manifesto for Manhattan* (New ed.). New York: Monacelli Press.
Kopp, A. (1967). *Ville et révolution: architecture et urbanisme soviétiques des années vingt* (1st ed.). Éditions Anthropos.
Lissitzky, E. (1929). *The reconstruction of architecture in the Soviet Union.*
Martí Arís, C. (2014). *Las variaciones de la identidad: Ensayo sobre el tipo en arquitectura* (Colección Arquia/temas, no. 36). Barcelona: Fundación Caja de Arquitectos.
Nietzsche, F. (1974). *The gay science.* Vintage Books.
Wilson, R., Lasala, J., & Sherwood, P. (2009). *Thomas Jefferson's academical village: The creation of an architectural masterpiece* (rev. ed.). Charlottesville: University of Virginia Press.

(Top) "Aéreo," Caio Barboza and Sofia Blanco Santos, Harvard GSD Superstudio, 2015–2016
(Bottom left) "A Stop on the Way," Caio Barboza and Sofia Blanco Santos, Harvard GSD Superstudio, 2015–2016
(Bottom right) Thermodynamics applied to high-rise and mixed-use prototypes, Huang Xiaokai, Harvard GSD, 2012

A Conversation with Andrés de Vandelvira

Francisco de los Cobos y Molina, Iñaki Ábalos, and Andrés de Vandelvira

Of all the literary genres used for the dissemination of architecture, the transcribed interview is without doubt the most popular. It combines ease of reading with a feel of veracity, of proximity, provided by the colloquial tone, not to mention the exposure of the personality that it implies. But we know that every professional interview is a gigantic rhetorical ruse with the aim of praising the individual, giving form to the fiction of thinking that a person knows what's happening, what needs to be done, and why. In fact, if people like interviews, to a large extent it is because they've been tinkered with, and because above the literal level of the words we discover that we make ourselves accomplices to their falsehoods, that they are an invitation to play and implicate ourselves. Nothing would be more boring than an honest interview with a working architect: complaints, doubts, imprecisions, whims, envies, and jealousies; everything that is usually omitted from the genre would probably occupy the entirety of the content.
The interview is a genuine literary genre of architecture, a technique for transmitting ideas, the rhetorical form par excellence for the beginning of the new millennium.

For this reason, confronted with the predicament of presenting the figure of Andrés de Vandelvira in an attractive manner, of presenting his thought and work as something endowed with a relative currency, I didn't hesitate to choose this rhetorical form. I must confess that in fact I did hesitate somewhat; in fact, I wrote this text in more conventional forms, which remained trapped in the web of time; the simple use of the past tense in the verbal forms thwarted all convincing efforts at achieving a sense of currency. So the two of us decided to transform the text, with its historicizing form, into a conversation about which all I can add in this introduction is that regardless of the effect this conversation might have on the reader, it contains the same information and analysis as in its previous, rigorously academic form; that it is no mere caprice; and that it contains as much truth as any of the interviews with architects they might have previously read.

> Iñaki Ábalos: Let's begin with your training. Your background was quite technical, and based on a certain familiarity with stonemasonry, which was rooted in the Gothic tradition …

Andrés de Vandelvira: That's certainly true. Though really, it is not a background that differs dramatically from that which many of the indisputable masters of Modernism have, such as Mies van der Rohe. But like him, I had the luck of surrounding myself from an early point with people with an intellectual background that was more elevated, which made me see other ways of tackling things. I think what was decisive for me—and for Mies—was accepting this other way of thinking about architecture without ever renouncing my more material or constructive knowledge at any point. Or rather, I sought to unite both forms of knowledge, one artisanal and the other abstract, which was arriving from Italy. Some of us felt that the socio political and economic changes we were living through were causing us to reconnect with the humanist concerns of the classical world, of the Romans. Seeing ourselves in them meant exploring a world that was at once new and connected with the past: a genuine intellectual adventure. I'll tell you, if there is one thing I am proud of, it's having understood that this was the historical context, and that in that context, the figure of the architect had to change. My main preoccupation was in reconciling the techniques learned from our ancestors with the new objectives of humanism, and in doing so, lending an original and specific meaning—a contextual one, if you like—to this revolution in thought we were destined to live through.

> IA: I agree with your assessment. For us, Vandelvira is associated first and foremost with the invention of a new conception of what it means to be an architect, and of adapting to the local situation through a pragmatic approach, though this adaptation does not mean renouncing anything or losing tension, but rather the contrary, a truly ambitious understanding of the job of being an architect. But you used a word, "contextual," which recently has gone from being quite fashionable to being almost completely forgotten in an incredibly brief period of time, even though some people still defend its use, at least in a broader sense. Can you describe to us what that word means to you, and the impact it had on your work?

AV: I happened to be working in an exciting context, in Andalusia, mainly in the country around Jaén, in a region

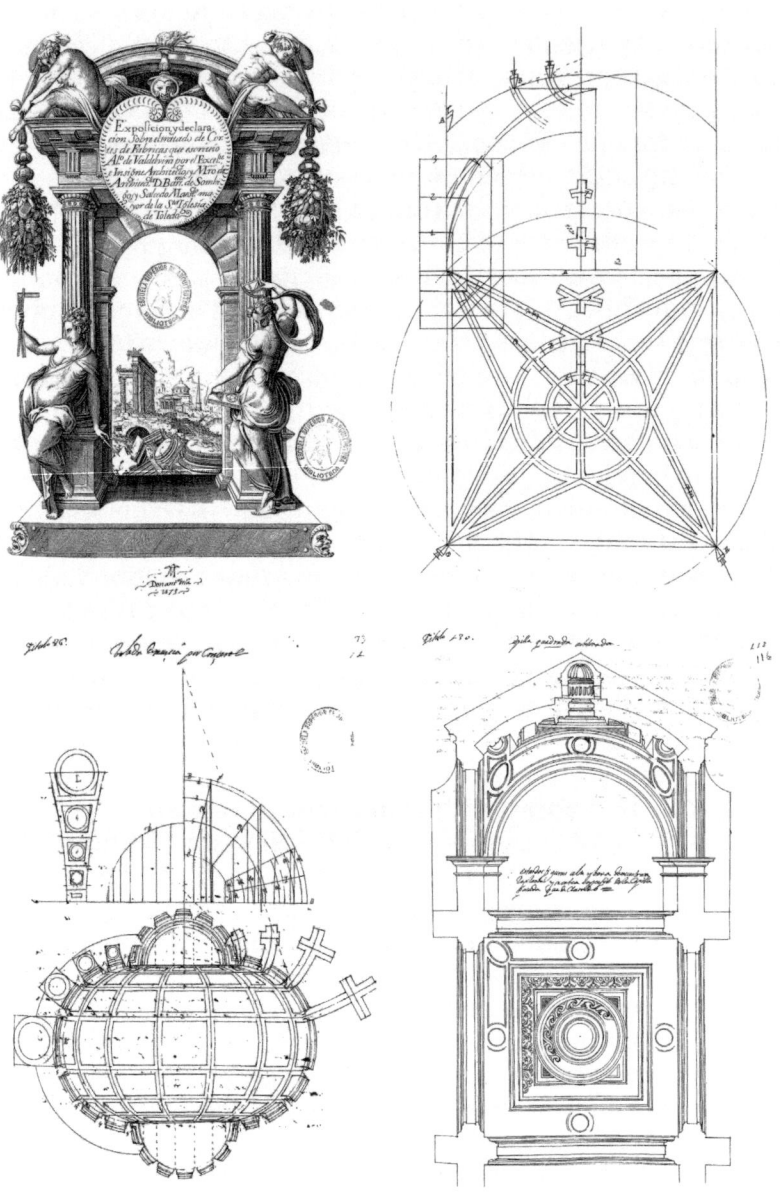

Title page and illustrations from *Libro de las traças de los cortes de la piedra*, Alonso de Vandelvira, ca. 1591

which just a few generations earlier had passed from Muslim hands to Christian ones, close to the center of Christianity at that time in Granada, which was a region with a fabulous architectural and artisanal tradition, with a number of techniques imported from the Flemish—sometimes people have wanted to see my surname as a Castilian adaptation of a Flemish name, and the only thing I'll say about that is that it pleases me greatly, even though its rigor is somewhat dubious. But I'll set the scene for you: It was a unique time and place, in which a new vernacular had to be invented by mixing Muslim architecture with the knowledge and technological advances of Gothic aesthetics to achieve certain objectives and ideals that were connected with the classical world, the Romans, and this in a region where they had been as influential as the Muslims had been—and where their traces were still highly visible, as in the columns of the Mezquita in Córdoba, for example. There were three highly distinct and sophisticated living cultures that formed a broader cultural context, as it were. And in case that wasn't enough, I had the great fortune of working for the secretary to the emperor on the redesign of Úbeda, his native village, transforming it into a true humanist city, a model and emulation of a true royal Renaissance court. And I left behind the complete designs of a cathedral for Jaén that, although I wasn't able to complete it, is one of the first major constructions in which the hand of a single author—the architect—is inscribed, something unheard of at the time, which thanks to the use of new methods such as scale models, was able to be brought to completion.

Certainly, the context in which I worked was extraordinarily rich in all senses of the word, and it provided me with not only resources for creating a kind of architecture that fed on all manner of stimulus, but also the opportunity to leave a reflection of my vision of the architecture of the city and of the architect as no other contemporary was able to do. I think that not having been a contextualist in such a situation would have been tantamount to being blind. I was conscious of the privilege that working under these conditions and with these sources implied, and my objective as an architect was to provide a faithful reflection of this truly global, integrative standpoint. As well as this, there were my companions along the way and my teachers, Diego de Siloé with the Granada Cathedral and Pedro Machuca with the royal palace in the Alhambra. Both figures were gifted with astounding abilities, and returned from Italy with a body of knowledge that was completely au fait with the ideals of the Renaissance. We were not isolated, and we were an empire in expansion, to a certain extent the center of Christianity; in fact, Siloé's Royal Chapel of Granada was an expression of this centrality.

That said, I should add that to walk past the Alhambra in Granada or the Mezquita in Córdoba and not be moved by their beauty, you'd have to be either an imbecile or a religious fundamentalist, and I have always been a practical man, a humanist, full of life and as open as possible. In fact, I saw the various cultures that coexisted there architecturally as different tectonic and material systems, and I did with them what I felt was most appropriate and pertinent, combining them until I found a system that was specific to our time which was in part an amalgam, in part an original idea that would implicate my oeuvre in an eclecticism whose definition begins to lose meaning the broader it becomes, in the sense that it can come to describe all manner of design aesthetics and therefore ceases to be useful because of its universality. I would be fine with being called eclectic so long as all forms of architecture could be described in this way. But I would like to say that my architecture was a *mestizo* architecture, an architecture of the intersections and of a dialogue among cultures, of hybridization, to use another fashionable term. I know that this can get somewhat excessive, but I don't have a better explanation to describe my career: ultimately it was a transition from learning a very concrete craft to the integration of new and ancestral cultures that were here and made up a unique landscape that called me to enter into a dialogue with it.

IA: The dogmatic precision and abstraction of the Modernists lacks sense in a world of growing integration and complexity: in this context, I think the idea of integrative systems becomes more crucial, more adequate, given that you speak of your work as a transition. We could begin to speak about some of your works, of your beginnings, and how you became conscious of the need to reinvent the figure of the architect. Your first works—with which you achieved the esteem that gave you access to bigger commissions—have been framed by some authors within the realm of the Plateresque, an affiliation which for some is carried on in the Chapel of the Savior in Úbeda.

Double columns and sail vaults in Hospital de Santiago, Úbeda
Detail of a column and capital in the Church of the Immaculate Conception in Huelma, Jaén

AV: First of all, I'd like to say that I've never really understood the attempts to see in my works a relationship to Plateresque aesthetics typical of the imagery of a retable in the style of Berruguete, for example. I was never a sculptor but essentially a builder, and my initial specialty was more in resolving construction problems than developing ornamental solutions, although obviously at the start of my career my references were very local, and I built in accordance with the fashions of the time, if you like. I landed in my true profession thanks not just to the training I received but also to the faith and generosity shown toward me by Diego de Siloé. Thanks to Siloé—who also had a background in the stonemasonry workshops of Flemish artisans who emigrated southward to the Kingdom of Spain, which at the time was experiencing a construction boom—I was able to imagine other ways of approaching architecture.

Siloé had had the opportunity to build in Italy, and what he was doing in Granada was simply fascinating and unique, and I would never have been able to dream up the things he was doing on my own. He had completed Egas's Gothic nave of the Granada Cathedral in the classical style with an astonishing level of skill, inventing solutions for the columns and the architraves and the lighting that would become hallmarks in the Andalusian architecture of the epoch. As well as this, though, he was constructing a central temple that emulated the one in Jerusalem, with a verve and a grandeur that were truly revolutionary. Nobody had ever seen anything like this, not to mention the construction solutions, the central arch, which unites the nave and the chapel; that is, topics that are well known to any aficionado of architecture. I learned a great deal both from his ability to resolve a pre existing problem—the nave—and from his audacity in adding a new floor to the construction.

In Úbeda, Francisco de los Cobos y Molina offered him the chance to complete a funerary chapel, the Capilla del Salvador (Chapel of the Savior). It was evident that Cobos wanted a miniaturized replica not just of the royal pantheon in Granada but also of the nave for churchgoers, and Siloé suggested a clever mixed solution, combining a nave and a central dome, which he entrusted to me since he could not see to its execution. For all the iconographic motifs I collaborated with Esteban Jamete, a Frenchman whose mastery of the human figure and classical symbolism was unrivaled. Thus, I was able to work with the security

Vaults of the sacristy in the Chapel of the Savior in Úbeda
Floor plan of the Chapel of the Savior in Úbeda

Corner entrance to the sacristy of the Chapel of the Savior in Úbeda
Human figures in the sacristy of the Chapel of the Savior in Úbeda

of the supervision and basic designs of a master, and the inestimable assistance of an exceptional sculptor of religious images. I felt like the conductor of an orchestra, and as such, felt the pleasure of being an architect in the new sense: the bare outline of the score was from Siloé and the virtuoso instrumentalist was Jamete, but its integration and organization, giving it form and meaning, those were my responsibilities. I took the opportunity presented by the sacristy—which emerged during the work—to organize the various pieces or monuments in a complex fashion. I conceived of the dome in the Roman style, with coffering, though the construction technique was a modification of the Gothic crossing vault, which was something I had already mastered. In the sacristy I organized a classical space based around three linked vaults. Since I had Jamete at my disposal—a singular individual, excessive, very free—I wanted the human figure to meld with the architecture, in order to celebrate the humanist return to material life, and used figurative resources and caryatids to join the walls and the ceiling … As a gesture, I placed a doorway in the corner of the sacristy, which is perhaps a little dramatic, but back then it was surprising, and gave a sense of my ambition.

> IA: The use of the human figure in the Vázquez de Molina Palace, in the attic, is also very singular. I'd like to talk about this palace and your intentions in creating it, about how it relates to the city and the space in front of the Chapel of the Savior. Rafael Moneo wrote about it some time ago with admiration, and remarked on the quality of the design—how contemporary it feels, and the intelligence of its incorporation into the design of the city surrounding it.

AV: The civil palace was another great opportunity, since it was largely a new program. There were no longer any enemies, and the idea of a fortress—in Granada, Machuca was transforming the Alhambra for the emperor, constructing a new palace—or of an *alcázar* (castle) no longer made any sense. The building that I erected concluded the northern end of the urban fabric of Úbeda, and the southern end opened up a gorgeous agricultural corridor, as well as extending the public antechamber that existed in front of the Chapel of the Savior … I couldn't resist the temptation of positioning it facing toward the south, with the expansive vistas this offered—which without

Main façade, Vázquez de Molina Palace, Úbeda

Aerial view of the city of Úbeda, showing the fabric of the city, in which plazas and buildings are woven together. The image shows the Chapel of the Savior, Vázquez de Molina Palace and Plaza, Town Hall Plaza, and Palace of Vela de los Cobos

a doubt was an entirely new vision—and toward this public space, creating with this orientation a classical façade, in accordance with the manuals that I had at my disposal, finished off with an attic with oculi and caryatids concealing a wooden roof in the Mudéjar style. This façade is a genuine celebration of the advent of a new and shining era, and everything in it has a festive character, while at the same time having a gravity that corresponds to the classic ideal. The façade was no longer defensive or an allegory of the afterlife, but communicated with the surrounding physical reality. The interior is joined together by a patio that I wanted to endow with a graceful and local character, using extremely slender proportions, with *nazarí* (Nasrid) influences, in a *quattrocentista* vernacular. I have always been interested in this extraordinarily beautiful fusion of exterior and interior, so full of fragility and vitality, and I think it is a scheme that is perfectly suited to the environmental characteristics of Andalusia, and as such, the palace is also an attempt at reconciling both ideals, the Roman, Vitruvian house, and the *nazarí* palace.

> IA: You created a great many other private works in Úbeda, as well as other public interventions ... How did you approach the city? Did you have any references in mind, Renaissance theories of architecture, for example?

AV: To be honest, my way of understanding the city was far removed from the idealism of the utopian cities of the Renaissance. Who knows whether I would have considered something like that in a newly founded city, for example in America, if I had been presented with the opportunity. But my predisposition has always been one of intervening in the topography, with no ordering plan that hierarchizes the totality. In this sense, I feel disconnected from all academic ideas—including those of Le Corbusier—and close to current forms of approaching the city through fragments. The Úbeda that I was able to help construct was not some educated imposition on top of what already existed there, but a coexistence of both. Some palaces I completed in an emphatically Roman style, but in others, the characteristics of the site or the program of the building pushed me to reach for more ambiguous solutions, concentrating on isolated problems like corners, the appearance of a decorative gallery, the entrance, or the patio, seeking to give new responses to questions that existed

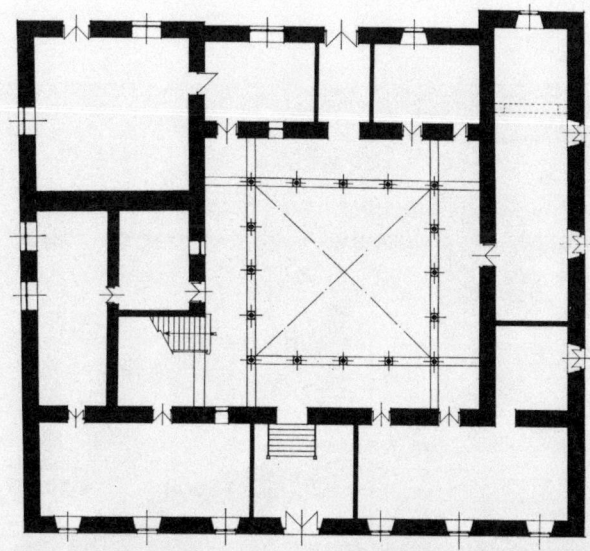

Floor plan of the Vázquez de Molina Palace, drawn by Fernando Chueca Goitia
Interior patio of the Vázquez de Molina Palace, image taken by Fernando Chueca Goitia

External view of the Palace of Vela de los Cobos, Úbeda, with its characteristic corner balconies

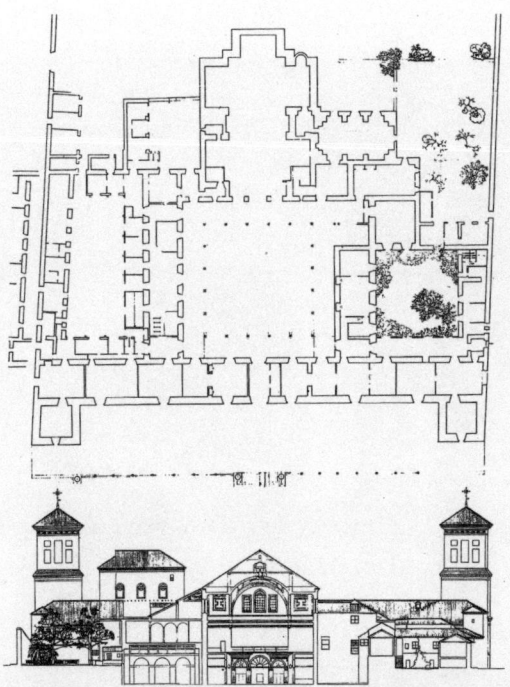

Plan and elevation of the Hospital de Santiago in Úbeda, drawn by Andrés Perea
Aerial view of the Hospital de Santiago in Úbeda

Interior of the Church of the Immaculate Conception in Huelma, Jaén

in the local and Plateresque traditions. In this way, I introduced aspects of the new architecture and material quality—something that was very important for me—making minor changes in scale without tearing the fabric, like fragments that could only be incorporated into a unified composition mentally.

This manner of integrating the city—which I know is quite relevant to you—brought me to a more broken-down working method, with each section afforded an autonomous meaning, taking shape in a dialogue with the stimuli of the city, or with the character of the program, with each part developing in the vernacular that best suits it. The method was shocking but productive, and although back then it might have seemed anti classical to some, it went on to have—as I'm sure you know—great success among architects, for example during the Enlightenment. And even today, it is surely one of the most widespread ways of interpreting the relationships between programs and the fabric of the city. Perhaps it is due to this conventionality it later acquired that it is difficult to now appreciate what was so daring about it then, so audacious and experimental.

> IA: In this sense, I think that the Hospital de Santiago in Úbeda is exemplary, because it repeats some of the themes we have mentioned, although in a more striking fashion …

AV: Yes, the hospital is a work of private philanthropy, a novel humanist gesture, but it could not have a celebratory or mundane character, like the palace. That's why its exterior is much more severe. You have to keep in mind that at the time, hospitals understood as places of transition to eternal life. The patio is the antechamber to the church; it is in these two spaces where there is an intensification of the formal richness of a spatial experience that culminates in the vaults of the church as a representation of the kingdom of heaven. Its interior responds to a thread of humanist logic, while its volume and exterior have a clearly Arabesque appearance, if you like, towers and volumes of great gravity, with an extremely restricted number of empty spaces, although its spatial organization is very conceptual and has all the elements, I think, of the architecture of the Renaissance, although perhaps in a dismembered way; the distinctive façade, the patio, the stairwell, organized as a logical sequence of spaces.

It has been compared to Bramante's Palazzo dei Tribunali, and I assure you that I myself find that both respond to a new urban and spatial order, although in my case the feeling of unity is diluted, as it were, in favor of other demands.

> IA: The use of ornament here is also more measured and intentional: the chapel is practically naked; even in the embellishing of the walls almost the only trace of a classical language that remains is in the entablatures, and even these have elements with an Islamic feel.

AV: Yes, it's true, as I advanced in my career I grew more conscious of the fact that my interpretation of the classical ideal was not ornamentalist but was based on an understanding of spaces and their union with coherent constructive systems. Due to its character, the hospital could never be anything but severe, but it was also revolutionary in its typology and spatial order. Some people have seen in it a precursor to the spatial arrangement of El Escorial, and that pleases me immensely. But it also has archaic elements, allusions to the great hospitals of the Catholic Monarchs of Spain, such as the one in Toledo. It seemed logical to me to use these elements—for example the impost that runs along the façade—like citations that reinforced its meaning. I think that in this building, I found a very liberating mode of working in which the three traditions or stimuli I wanted to learn from or use to give form to a system of construction melded together without being resolved into a system of continuity.

> IA: We still haven't spoken of the sail or handkerchief vault, which is without a doubt the keystone of your system of spatial and structural arrangement. We could do that in order to introduce your magnum opus, the Jaén Cathedral, or the Chapel of the Benavides in Baeza, which repeats in part the Chapel of the Savior, but with a greater degree of liberty, as it is not conditioned by any kind of trace from the past.

AV: The sail vault is nothing but a transformation of medieval cross vaults, which elegantly resolved the issue of covering the system of cruciform pillars or columns which Diego de Siloé conceived in the nave of the Cathedral of Granada. In the Chapel of the Benavides, I felt that I had a

Conversation with Andrés de Vandelvira

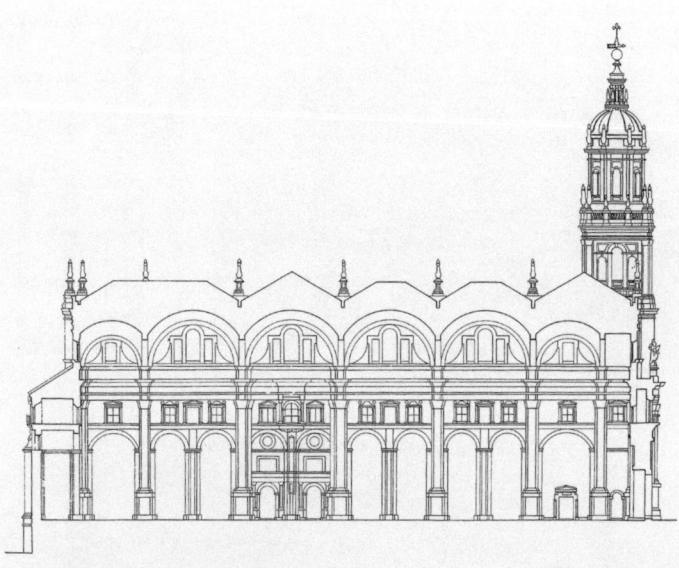

Longitudinal section of the Jaén Cathedral
Sail vaults in the Jaén Cathedral

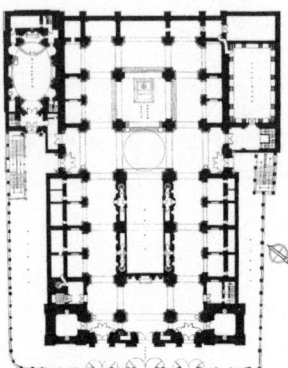

View of Jaén and the cathedral in its urban environment
Floor plan of the Jaén Cathedral drawn by Fernando Chueca Goitia
View of the central nave of the Jaén Cathedral

unique opportunity to synthesize the two parts of Siloé's great project, a temple with a central floor and a nave, using a unique construction system. In contrast to the dome on pendentives or the coffering of the Chapel of the Savior, which required singular operations, my invention delivered simplicity and continuity (though not only this). I believe that the sail vault also has a certain degree of weightlessness and continuity with the arches between columns, which make this solution more fitting and elegant. I'm fascinated by this idea of weightlessness, which in principle does not correspond to the solidity and tectonic nature of Roman architecture.

Perhaps it would be relevant here to mention the attraction that I felt toward *nazarí* architecture, even though in my opinion it is not at odds with classical ideals. A sign of that is the spatial sensitivity of the civil architecture of Brunelleschi, for example, who in some ways can claim to have been the one to incorporate it into the architecture of the Renaissance when he used it in the Ospedale degli Innocenti. But on top of this, the natural feeling that it gives to the join between the wall and the column bestows a very "liberal" spatiality, if you'll permit me to use that term. In my previous attempts in Huelva, for example, I saw clearly that civil space was paradoxically moving away from the mysticism of the Gothic era and that the ecclesiastical space was moving toward the civil space. I have never been religious in the traditional sense nor a proponent of the Counter-Reformation, and my interest in religious architecture lacks any element of veneration. I'll put it this way: with my religious themes, I wanted to be more Velázquez than Valdés Leal.

IA: You must have done something right with it, given that these ceilings had such success after your use of them. And I'm not referring so much to the fact that for quite some time it became the canonical solution employed in the Andalusian Renaissance—for example in Malaga, in the sacristy in Seville, etc.—but to its repeated use by architects working in completely different temporal and geographic contexts, such as in the work of John Soane, which, be it in his own house or the Bank of England, abounded in these weightless and civil qualities. We also find it in the work of Edwin Lutyens, and I would even go so far as to say that it is a precursor to Guastavino's patents—realized with bricks—which were so successful in the United States, and are intrinsically linked with the classicism that McKim, Mead & White strove for. The English called it a "pendentive," alluding to its sense of suspension (Alberti called it *en vela*, or sail-like), and it's true that it hangs in suspension, as in the recent example proposed and constructed by Juan Navarro Baldeweg in Salamanca.

AV: I'm interested in the expression *en vela*, because it really does behave as if the space were inflating the stone severies between the transverse arches that support them. And on that, I would like to add that it encompasses the load by proposing its inversion. In the empirical method and in the lightness and plasticity that it seeks to convey, I do think there is a similarity that I think is worth underscoring.

IA: I agree, especially if we think of the Jaén Cathedral. But I would be interested in returning to your position on the matter of dealing with religious commissions with a stance that is really not very Counter-Reformist at all. I'm not going to ask you to define yourself publicly, as I know that it wouldn't make sense right now (and given the balancing acts that one had to perform in your time when it came to these questions), but from the texts you read and the company you kept—like Esteban Jamete, who ended up in the hands of the Inquisition—we can deduce a certain Erasmist spirit, trusting more in individual forces, in work, and in one's own conscience about our individual acts than in the religious rules and norms handed down by the Vatican. On this point, I believe that your attitude bears parallels to your attitude toward classical norms, which you saw as a point of reference but not a set of laws. I think that this spirit is alive in the Jaén Cathedral, whose character of being a civil salon links this work more with a Gothic marketplace, like those in Valencia or in Palma, than with any church or cathedral. This allows it to move away from the transitional solutions of Gothic or Renaissance architecture, as well as reducing the directionality of the space …

AV: Yes, yes, it's true that its form is that of a grand salon and this singularity pleases me enormously, even though in part it was a result of not wanting to have to increase the height of the main nave and in part due to causes that had nothing to do with me, since it served to incorporate the edge of the preexisting wall, which impeded all possibility of a circular apse. This position on the edge of the Arab city and built over its vestiges was a major influence in determining not only the form but also the character that I wanted to confer to the cathedral, a hybrid between a palace, a fort, and a basilica, to speak in simplified terms. The wall that I proposed was not particularly modulated, and had a single system of openings in the form of windows, balconies, and oculi, while the Serlian windows that illuminate the principal nave were set further back. In the interior, with the even height of the naves, this market-like character is underscored, establishing a unique and continuous entablature and producing an encompassing, clearly civil façade around the same interior, with windows and balconies, creating an effect that for me almost calls to mind an urban space, a plaza faced by the impressive façades of the public buildings. Of course I am trying to explain these things in a language that is comprehensible today. Back then, these themes were not so evident.

> **IA:** I have no doubt that you are making a real effort to communicate here. In any case, I don't think that this is something unusual for you in your trajectory as an architect. I think of the treatise you wrote and illustrated with your son, and it seems clear to me that this dialogical effort forms an intrinsic part of your understanding of architecture and the role of the architect.

AV: I hadn't thought about it in those terms, but perhaps I agree with your assessment. As I said at the outset of this conversation, my intent was to collaborate in the transformation and elevation of the intellectual and social status of the architect. The secrecy of the master stonemasons was a vestige of the Middle Ages that was inadmissible in a world in which knowledge had begun to circulate freely through civil society. At the same time, though, given my background and training, my contribution could not be conceptual, like that of Alberti, but rather technical. There were also instruments such as a nascent, descriptive geometry, coinciding with the creation of large models that had already allowed for the transmission of traditional techniques, and for the avoidance of the situation in which every new master had to start their works from scratch according to their own criteria. The model that I had fabricated for Jaén, along with the support of my building engineer, was central to the fact that the Jaén Cathedral was completed as a unified work. It might seem entirely banal to us today, but the fabrication of such a model was a genuine revolution, and Jaén, despite some confused elements, is perhaps the only cathedral that responds to a unique and overarching project, even though I was only able to commence it and provide the guidelines, pushing the vocation of the architect toward something higher.

Coming up with simplified construction systems that would efficiently resolve the problems was the second part of the question. I wrote a book that was supposed to hand down my knowledge to the following generations, naturally with an altruistic aim, but also a selfish one. I set things out in a way that sought to do away with a conception of architecture that was like a puzzle in which redoing what had already been done often took just as long—or even longer—than completing it the first time. That was my strategy and I think, in a general sense, I was successful.

> IA: Listening to you talk about yourself, I can't help but think again of the figure of Mies. Setting aside the obvious differences between the two of you, he also made an effort to connect the perception of space with a technical system of great simplicity, universal in principle and globally applicable, although of course you can always tell when his hand is involved …

AV: Let me tell you, this revolution came from the hand of Juan Bautista de Toledo, and, if you like, of Juan Herrera in the construction of the Monastery of El Escorial. That is where prefabrication was really invented, giving way to a drastic change in construction conditions. I left the instruments allowing the work to be faithfully interpreted and transmitted in such a way that the outcome would be unitary, even if the construction lasted 300 years. But by introducing new techniques in cutting and laying the stone, they abolished the need for the works to endure eternally (even though the generous financial support of the crown was certainly another essential aspect). They made

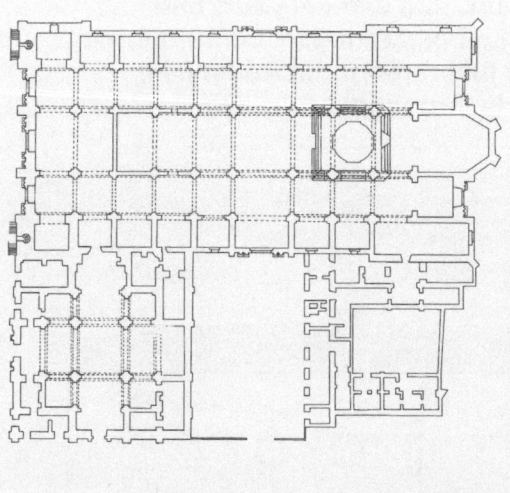

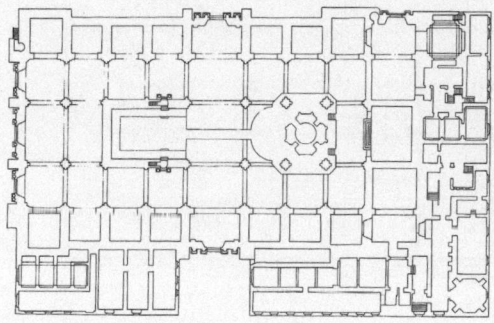

Floor plans of the cathedrals of Mexico City (top) and Puebla (bottom)
Cathedrals of Jaén, Mexico City, and Puebla (from top to bottom)

possible my effort at creating a form that was truly revolutionary, and you could almost say that modern construction began there.

IA: Nevertheless, that work of yours had enormous influence, lasting for centuries and extending not just throughout Andalusia, but particularly throughout America.

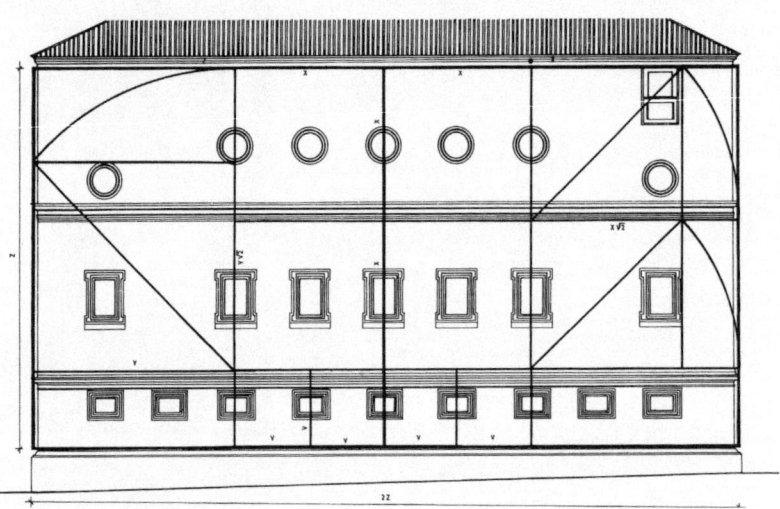

Elevation of the sacristy of the Jaén Cathedral

AV: Yes, perhaps El Escorial was too singular to generate implications of a collective nature. In this sense, my work always had a preoccupation with utility and flexibility. I was interested in establishing a relationship between formal types and construction techniques, between topography and the memory of place, and in attending to the character of the program as the Picturesque and Romantic authors later did. I have been a desk architect, someone whose work consists in thinking and sketching at a table, something unusual in my time, but which for me represented the most intense element of my profession, because this effort of maturation that one needs in order to confront problems abstracted of all contingency brings solutions that are at once general and particular. Solutions that can be used by others in the same way that I used earlier ones. I always believed that architecture was an art form whose themes could be applied in various circumstances, that through architecture, a cultural dialogue can be established. The fact that the book I wrote with the indispensable support of my son coincides thematically with that of Philbert de l'Orme—even though obviously because of the surrounding circumstances his received a much greater response—corroborates this understanding of the vocation. For this reason as well, I have to say that one of the works of which I am most proud is the suite formed by the Zócalo and the cathedrals of Mexico City and Puebla. Obviously I am not the material creator of these great works, but I do believe that my ideas are present in them. And not just because their designs reproduce those of Jaén to a significant degree, but also because of the urban conception of the ensemble. I think the Zócalo is the great public space that the Spaniards left in America, and see its enormous, truly fantastic scale as the product of placing Renaissance ideas in relation with the monumental scale of the Aztec city. I like to think that I would have attempted to do something similar, just as I did in Andalusia with the *nazarí* influences. That is the kind of dialogue I'm talking about. And allow me to add that this reference to the churches of America ties in with your earlier remark about globalization as a phenomenon of your time. As you can see, not only did we import ideas from the north of Italy, we were also capable of constructing unique works on other continents, something that many people see as being particular to the recent turn of the millennium.

> IA: We've left the work of the sacristy of the Jaén Cathedral, which you were able to conceive and construct yourself, till last. In my opinion, it is one of the most beautiful works of architecture that has been created in our country, not just during the Renaissance, but in any era.

AV: I really appreciate the compliment. It is also the work that provided me with the most satisfaction. Being a product of my later years, it is the one that best encapsulates my thinking, and is the most balanced. It is the most balanced in part because in it, all the demands that I have mentioned over the course of this interview are present, the extraordinarily

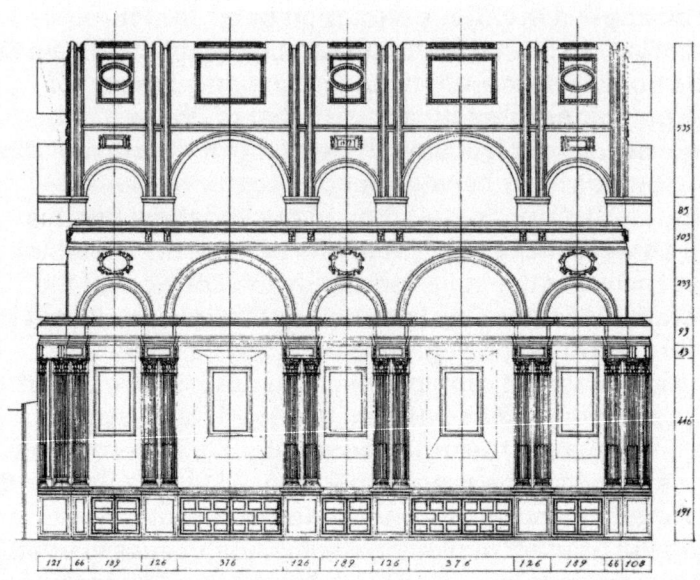

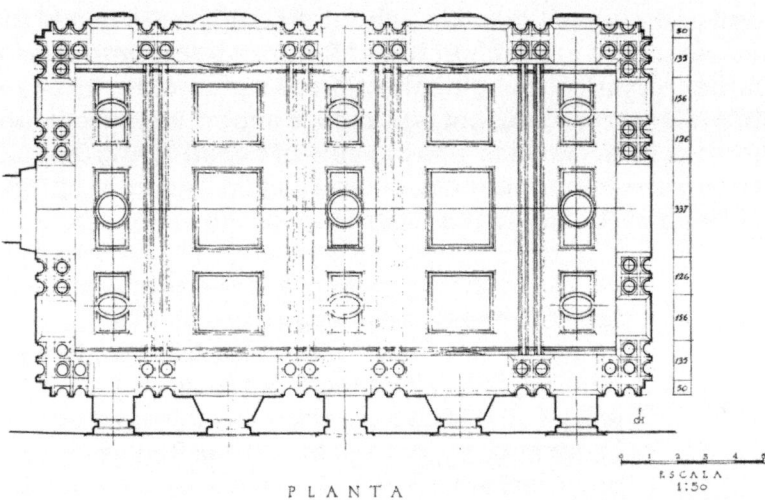

Section and floor plan of the sacristy of the Jaén Cathedral

intricate stonework, the Roman aesthetics, a certain Moorish, almost Byzantine spatiality ...

> IA: People often see in the solution of the double arch a reference to the Mezquita in Córdoba, almost superimposed over the Court of the Lions of the Alhambra, or over Bramante or the Sistine Chapel ...

AV: The sacristy needed volume in its walls so that accommodating the chest of drawers would not disrupt the space, so for this prosaic reason I decided to use a free-standing system of double columns, with its central columns in the wall and an A-B-A rhythm that organizes the space around a central axis. All this produced a spatial arrangement in which the arches and the barrel vault entered into a sort of resonance whose ornamental richness combined with the double columns was closer to the Court of the Lions of the Alhambra than to other Renaissance sources, of which I was perfectly conscious. I wanted to lend a spatial character to that richness of volumes obtained by the multiplication of columns and rhythms (which I learned from the Alhambra), a sense of overflow, by covering it and converting it into an interior. The doubled arches permitted me not just to lighten and concentrate the loads, but also to establish that correspondence between wall and vault. The doubled nature of the arches is also a play on that of the columns. The motif of the double arch was not present only in the Mezquita, it was also in the aqueducts of Mérida, for example. Ultimately, at all points I utilized what today we might dub a double vernacular that could be interpreted in both a Moorish and a Roman key, in order to obtain the ornamental richness of the former with a more technical —or stereotomic—style. That is what I attempted to achieve with this space.

> IA: I'd like to tell you an anecdote, if that's okay. I had visited your sacristy various times and never understood the reasons behind its attractiveness, its ambiguity, as you yourself have mentioned. During a trip with colleagues, including José Ignacio Linazasoro, we were able to visit the Mezquita in Córdoba, the sacristy, and the Jaén Cathedral on consecutive days. Thanks to the efforts of Linazasoro we had a revelatory experience in being able to enjoy these works

Interior of the sacristy of the Jaén Cathedral

without the aid of artificial light, which without a doubt is necessary today for tourist visits, but which modifies—often quite drastically—the original spatial and perceptual conditions. The Mezquita, especially in the original sections, where hardly any openings for overhead lighting were made, is impressive under an oblique light coming from the façades, leaving the ceilings in complete darkness. The double arcade is extremely fine and only tenuously perceptible, causing the ceiling to disappear, which on the other hand is far less elaborate, which makes sense, given that it remained hidden from sight. The following day, the effect that we were able to see in the sacristy was equally unique. Surprisingly, the light does not come from above, even though the wall allows it without problems; rather, it comes from gaps created by the intercolumniations along the side of the sacristy facing the exterior façade (south).

AV: Indeed, this double arcade would have allowed "Roman" light to enter the sacristy; that is, overhead light, similar to in a Roman bath. The effect obtained in this way is that of an enormous heterodoxy, Roman spaces bathed in Muslim light … I chose horizontal light, oblique light, a light whose effects on the circular columns and the classic molding certainly is not orthodox.

It's an acute observation, and I don't know if I can say whether it was conscious or not, but in any case it serves to exemplify what my interests were, and the idea of beauty to which I aspired. An atmosphere of weightlessness by way of the inversion of the usual order of the shadows cast due to the reflection of the light on the surface of the floor. There is nothing more beautiful for a creator than hearing new interpretations of what one was trying to produce; regardless of whether they were present in the moment of conception, they are present in the work because they are alive in your head, and that is the most important thing.

Coda

Andrés de Vandelvira lived between 1505 and 1575. In his time, he was a great heterodox figure and a meticulous professional, orderly, hardworking, and passionate.
He brought about an enormous revolution from within an artisanal profession, establishing himself thanks to a certain amount of family support and the support of his masters. In all of this and in many other respects, he resembles that other great figure who in just a single generation would lend splendor to the court of Philip IV of Spain: Diego Velázquez, the figure who can best illustrate the meaning of a vocation and a career like that of Vandelvira. Both dignified the profession through their own social ascent and did not keep this objective private, but made it a central concern of their work. Both wanted to give artists the position and social status they deserved, refusing to remain at the level of the artisan as tradition would have had it. Both were initially trained in familiar styles—one in a meticulous, detail-oriented Plateresque aesthetic; the other in the anecdotal Tenebrism of Seville—that still bore the traces of the classical influences of the Flemish on Spanish artistic practices.

Both were technically flawless, the most skillful practitioners of their trades. But at the same time, both understood that their ability meant they were obliged to move forward. Both of them understood that this forward movement could only come from an immersion in the new humanist currents arriving from Italy. The two of them likewise sought and attained the patronage of high-ranking personalities and influential politicians—Velázquez in the court of Philip IV and Vandelvira with the secretary to the emperor, the person who controlled the commercial traffic with the Americas, and who aspired to establish his reputation as a humanist by leaving behind a Renaissance city in Úbeda. Both exhibited a new and extraordinary sensitivity for the human figure as a vehicle for expressing the new concerns in their respective arts. In both oeuvres, the human body was an expression of an interest in representing classical mythology, but both also did this in a characteristic way, identifying these mythic characters with civil society, naturalizing them, thus moving toward a characteristic vision of Spanish art in the face of the imported classicist idealism.

What is true of the human figure is also true of Vandelvira's use of architectural orders, a canon he was familiar with, but respected and observed with a high degree of liberty, using more slender proportions when he wanted to achieve new effects. In both men there is an intense necessity to express the emergence of a civil society in the face of the medieval monopoly of religion over intellectual life. We know how Velázquez managed to avoid the kind of specialization in religious themes that was virtually obligatory in his epoch—due to the system of imperial patronage—and became accepted as the painter of the king; but it is no less true that Vandelvira was an architect of civil palaces, hospitals, and urban spaces. An urban architect, if you will, even if the themes that he dealt with had religious content. The palatial elevation of the interior walls of the Jaén Cathedral—including their arrangement and luminosity, as was mentioned earlier—abounds in this heterodox and singular idea of a conception of architecture that is eminently civil and urban. For Vandelvira as for Velázquez, maturity brought with it a synthesis in which all the demands and stimuli that had formed part of their education were present.
At the same time, both were divesting their work of all that was superfluous in order to achieve an apparent naturalness and simplification that conceals their impressive mastery of their vocations. Both of them left two interiors as their masterpieces—that of the Royal Palace in *Las Meninas* for Velázquez, and the sacristy of Jaén for Vandelvira—in which it is easy enough to find more than one analog, certainly in the spatial depth and the mastery of the human figure and the proportions, in their capacity and respective interest in imbuing the air around the figures with a new density and vitality, an idea whose audacity would only be appreciated after a significant period of time had passed. Velázquez and Vandelvira were also pioneers in incorporating the landscape into their work. Just like Velázquez in his Italian paintings or in the backgrounds of his works hanging in El Prado that have become so associated with him, it is easy to recognize in Vandelvira a spirit with a real feel for the beauty of the landscape that surrounded his works, be it natural or urban. In the attention he gave to landscapes in the outskirts of the city and to urban hierarchies, his careful topographic articulation is an unmistakable indication of the emergence of this sensitivity.

Of course, there would be no sense in comparing the quality of their respective oeuvres, and that is not the intention of this comparison, which has more in common with a portrayal of two "parallel lives" than an artistic analysis. What I'd like to emphasize here is the singularity and value of the

View of the Garden of Villa Medici, Diego de Velázquez, ca. 1630 or ca. 1649

individual himself, the significance of his work, the very fact—which was certainly unique at the time—that Vandelvira possessed a true and vital personal project superimposed over his professional one. It was not a matter of doing architecture in the manner of the classical world, rather that he also had a need to attain the individuality of a Renaissance artist, to reach a freedom on a par with the technical expertise that allowed him to construct his vision of the world. It is this consciousness of individuality in relation to the work, to the types and the urban designs, to the context and the dominant culture, that make Vandelvira a contemporary architect. He is a figure who is still appealing today, as is clearly reflected in the proliferation of studies in recent decades since Fernando Chueca's brilliant biography, made up of contributions not just by scholars but also by authors like Linazasoro, Tafuri, and Moneo, in which the historiographical interest cedes to the interest in what is current, what is vital about his architecture and his way of being an architect, because it speaks to us with surprising lucidity and relevance.

Bibliography:
Chueca Goitia, F. (1954). *Andrés de Vandelvira* (Artes y artistas). Madrid: Laboratorio de Arte de la Universidad de Sevilla, Instituto Diego Velázquez, del Consejo Superior de Investigaciones Científicas.
De Vandelvira, A. (2015). *Libro de trazas de cortes de piedras*. Madrid: Instituto Juan de Herrera.
De Vandelvira, A., Llimargas, M., & Palacio Provincial. (2007). *Vandelvira, Renacimiento del sur: 500 aniversario: exposición*, Jaén, January–March 2008, Salas Provinciales de Exposiciones, Palacio Provincial. Diputación Provincial de Jaén.
Pretel Marín, A. (2005). *Andrés de Vandelvira. V Centenario*. Albacete: Instituto de Estudios Albacetenses "Don Juan Manuel" de la Excma. Diputación de Albacete.

I would like to thank Eduardo Prieto, Juan Calatrava, and José Carlos Palacios for their suggested revisions to the original version of this text.

A Monstrous Encounter Between Transcendentalism and Positivism

Portrait of Frederick Law Olmsted in 1857

Act I: The Founding of Central Park

I will not recount in detail the story of how and why a nucleus of intellectuals came to demand the planning of a large-scale site of leisure for the citizens of New York, nor the historical vicissitudes that led to that demand culminating in the announcement and immediate execution of the great natural agora that is Central Park. Others have already done so brilliantly, and I shall defer to them.[1] Nevertheless, it is relevant to outline the confluence of disparate tendencies and ideologies—between a number of Unitarian and Congregationalist Protestants, the utopian socialist acolytes of Fourier, and the transcendentalists—that occurred at

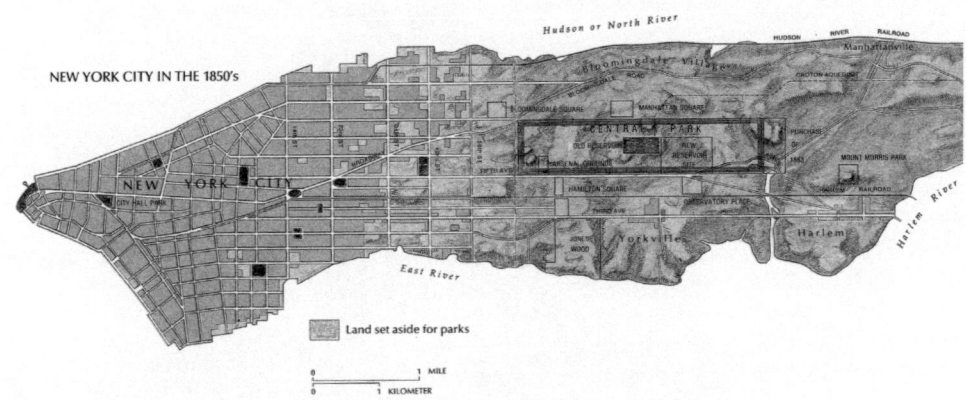

Manhattan in 1850

this particular moment, converging on a common interest. For all of these groups, the public park was viewed as an institution that represented the spirit of the new society, and it is this confluence that is the determining factor for the success of the operation.

The first aspect that needs to be acknowledged is that at the time, Central Park was not centrally located within the city of New York, but on the peninsula of Manhattan. If we observe the maps of the city in 1850 we see clearly that the chosen site is a long way from the urban center that had then established itself at Washington Square. Its ultimate location was the subject of lengthy discussions, and the final decision conformed more with practical and economic

1   See Rosenzweig, R. & Blackmar, E. (1994). *The park and the people: A history of Central Park*. Henry Holt and Company.

reasons than any other kind of considerations. The site of
Jones's Wood, already being utilized at the time as a variant of
the pleasure gardens of London on the southern banks of the

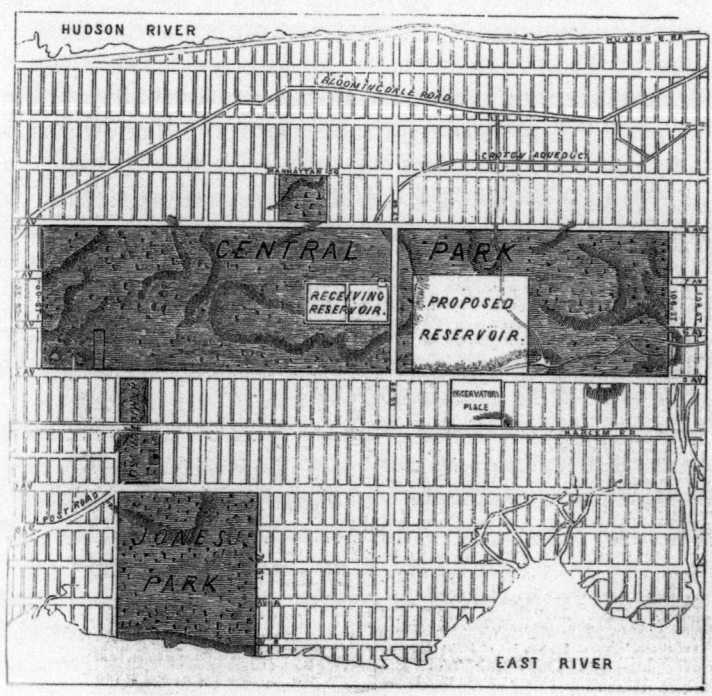

Map of the proposed locations for Central Park, 1852
Photograph taken in 1858 from Vista Rock of the area of the lake in the southeast

Thames—private gardens in which, for a fee, visitors
could spend the day in the fresh air, with dances, food, and
other attractions—offered natural features that were
much more attractive. Jones's Wood was adjacent to the river

and boasted fertile soils brimming with vegetation and woodlands. The eventual site of Central Park abandoned a proximity to the water—the vital element of the commercial activity of New York—and the terrain could not have been less fertile. When the topographical survey was carried out, it was revealed that due to the deforestation that had been necessary for port activities, the vegetal substrate was almost inexistent or minimal, with rocky ground in practically all sections, and because of the topographical configuration of the site, many areas were swampy, with no natural drainage, and there were little more than a few scrawny trees growing scattered across the entire site. The only reason for the choice of the site was that it was central to a peninsula across which, hypothetically, the grid of the great blocks of New York traced out in 1811 would extend in an unpredictable future, a virtual network from which a lot of grand dimensions was extracted (252 hectares) between Fifth and Eighth Avenues and between 59th and 106th Streets, whose proportions of 1:5 and rectilinear form, shaped by that network, fit poorly with—or perhaps even contradicted entirely—the prevailing Picturesque ideals. To cap it all off for the landscape architects, the only constructions that existed there were the city's reservoirs, hideous industrial constructions which occupied a central and dominant position, and which logically needed to be retained. In positioning the site in this way it was also necessary to guarantee transport connections between the east and west of the city in this area, obliging planners to allow the transversal passage of traffic on all sides, which hindered the desired spatial continuity of the site.

Despite all this and the attractiveness of Jones's Wood, the decision was made by the controversial mayor Fernando Wood (1812–1881), and an international design competition was launched. To ensure its success, Wood secured the participation of major European figures such as Jean-Charles Alphand and Joseph Paxton, which gives an idea of the preferences of those running the competition. But prior to this, perhaps as an extension of his responsibilities as the chief topographical engineer and commissioner of parks for the City of New York, Egbert Viele (1825–1902), who had been tasked with creating a topographical survey of the site, designed an initial projection of the park, which would be the ultimate catalyst for the announcement of the design contest, due to the criticisms that his design sparked from influential individuals such as Charles Elliott.

This design deserves our critical attention because not only did it provide the first visualization of the possibilities of the site, it also conveyed its complexity, with Viele's plan providing the contest with many of the specifications for the proposals, including the budget and practically all of the activities the park was expected to accommodate, along with the need for a new reservoir and four connections between Fifth and Eighth Avenues crossing the park. The specifications contained an area for parades and military processions (which in Viele's proposal, given his military background, had been disproportionately generous) three recreation areas, spaces reserved for livestock shows, a concert hall, a lake for ice-skating in winter, a flower garden, a large fountain, and a tower with a lookout platform, among other things.

Viele's project was defended by some, not so much for its quality as for its attention to the interests of the populace, since his design linked the project with the aforementioned pleasure gardens, permitting a republican and populist defense of a home-grown flavor, to combat a naturalist and civic conception that some then considered an aristocratic import from Europe. In order to deal with the disparity of the criteria, a commission was created that decided to identify a respected and trusted individual to pen a report on the matter. Calvert Vaux (1824–1895) was the man entrusted with the task. He was a young British architect who had arrived in the United States in 1850 to work with Andrew Jackson Downing (1815–1852), a landscape architect of great influence and a conduit between European landscape architecture and the nascent American discipline, who died tragically young and whom we cannot, unfortunately, discuss at length here. Familiar with the leading traditions of landscape architecture, having established himself in New York as an independent professional and gained access to local circles of influential individuals, Vaux announced a conclusive verdict: the design was inadequate. The reasons he provided were well argued. The design did not avoid the intrusion of traffic in the view of the landscape, disrupting any possible effect of continuity. It also lacked a totalizing artistic conception, failing to identify visual focal points or central spaces that would channel the movements of the viewer. Lacking lines of sight or distinguishing frames, the viewer would oscillate between monotony and confusion, unable to locate the "picture," with a complete lack of all established notions of the Picturesque. What's more, the design had not structured the use of vegetation to create the effect of distance and spaciousness, nor had it camouflaged the old reservoir, to which it had even added viewing platforms, in a flagrant lack of landscaping vision. The sophistication of Vaux's analysis reflected the education in the themes of Picturesque aesthetics that he had acquired while working alongside Jackson Downing. These themes had their origins in the aesthetic revolution that was brought about toward the end of the eighteenth century by English theorists such as Uvedale Price, Richard Payne Knight, and William Gilpin.

Around 1770 in England, nature was a purely visual material for which a highly structured and extremely "mechanized"

Calvert Vaux ca. 1860

system of knowledge had been developed, aimed at creating a sculptural composition, which through various combinations produced a certain harmony based on the smoothness of the relief, on the effects of depth and chromatic variety, and on the creation of effects and sensations of a psychological nature associated with specific presentations or "vistas." The absence of criteria beyond the pictorial is in itself evidence of the decisive influence of the fashion of landscape painting in the success of the English garden,[2] especially the landscapes of Claude Lorrain (1600–1682), Nicolas Poussin (1594–1665), and Salvatore Rosa (1615–1673), whose paintings serve as a model for compositions and frameworks that provided a vision of

2   Indeed, the word "landscape" in its visual sense entered the English language via the terminology of Dutch landscape painting.

the garden as corrected, idealized nature, imbued with meaning through ruins, mythological or religious figures, inscriptions, or even, as Horace Walpole did in 1747, through animals chosen for their color and form in order to achieve a desired pictorial effect—"some Turkish sheep and two cows, all studied in their colours for becoming the view."[3]

Sir Uvedale Price, portrait by Sir Thomas Lawrence, ca. 1799
Engraving by Thomas Hearne and Benjamin Thomas Pouncy for the poem *The Landscape* by Richard Payne Knight, 1794

For Uvedale Price, the Picturesque is something more complex, a wild, crude, and messy landscape, characterized by its variety and entanglement, more natural and more real than the pastoral or the sublime, halfway between one and the other, careless and confused at times, but which

[3] Walpole H. (1840). *The Letters of Horace Walpole: Earl of Orford.* Vol. 1 1735–1745. Richard Bentley, 529.

never ceases to surprise and pique our curiosity as we pass through it, offering us by turns flashes of a harmonic or pastoral beauty and scenes closer to the sublime. Price identifies "two of the most fruitful sources of human pleasure [...] variety [...] [and] intricacy, a quality which, though distinct from variety, is so connected and blended with it, that the one can hardly exist without the other. According to the idea I have formed of it, intricacy in landscape might be defined as that disposition of objects which, by a partial and uncertain concealment, excites and nourishes curiosity."[4]

While the contrast between pastoral beauty and the sublime supposes an antithetical aesthetic arrangement, the Picturesque introduces the idea of a transition, or, if you will, of dialectical synthesis, which allows for the articulation of pastoral episodes with more dramatic sections. Price's proposition originates from the acceptance of everyday landscapes as something worthy of admiration and observation. It supposes a new way of seeing that projects an empiricist valorization of the landscape which posits variety as the core of aesthetic pleasure.

In demanding surprise and variety, Price's Picturesque aesthetics introduce the idea of succession, and with it, of the duration of the aesthetic experience; something that demands a new technique, that of organizing space in time by way of linked sequences whose diverse effects are achieved by gathering a variety of resources from the assorted conceptions of pre existing landscape architecture, including a fascination for Chinese gardening, which was being discovered and admired at the time. Thus, the Picturesque brings together in practice the spectrum of aesthetic effects of the tradition of English landscape gardening, irregular and naturalist, developed in the early eighteenth century through the work of figures such as Alexander Pope, Lancelot "Capability" Brown, William Kent (1685–1748), and Humphry Repton (1752–1818), giving them a new meaning, incorporating new, relatively dramatic and irregular scenes and organizing them in a sequential spatial structure that demands of the landscape architect a number of skills, as much botanical as architectural and scenographic. All of these themes form the substrate of Calvert Vaux's critique, and this critique would go on to have decisive consequences in the international competition.

4   Price, U. (1794). *An essay on the picturesque as compared with the sublime and the beautiful.* Hereford. Extended at. (1810). *Essays on the picturesque.* Mawman, 21–22.

Act II: Winning Strategies

When the competition was announced, Calvert Vaux and Frederick Law Olmsted (1822–1903) entered into a partnership of convenience. Since his return to New York, Olmsted had been working under the direction of Viele, who was evidently unfazed by the rejection of his proposal. Olmsted asked Viele for permission to participate in the competition, and was thus in close contact with the municipal authorities. Vaux had demonstrated his knowledge and argumentative skill, increasing his authority in the eyes of the jury. The project that the two would propose possessed a great sense of strategic cunning in not departing too much—if anything, more the contrary— from the directives of Viele's project—who at the end of the day was an influential municipal functionary—while subtly incorporating corrections responding to all the points identified in Vaux's report. In fact, the project could be understood as a revision that incorporated the technical insights of the Picturesque into a project—Viele's—that was conceptually close to the pleasure garden but lacked technique and vision.

This hybrid character announced a certain disregard for the stylistic orthodoxy of the time as well as Olmsted's knack for pulling together and selling hybrid propositions. As architects who have participated in such competitions would well know, all of these strategies are legitimate, and they usually—though not always—have a good chance of success. On top of this, the project was presented exquisitely.

Sketched out in color by Calvert Vaux, the proposal was accompanied by different views and a text of great persuasive force written by Olmsted. The project demonstrated, as it were, the confidence of its authors and their desire to convince the jury that this confidence was entirely justified. The proposal represented a highly advanced display of persuasive techniques for its time, more at home in the current context than the traditional one, including renderings, color illustrations, strategic arguments accompanying the images ... But beyond these strategic questions, the project had two firm bases: one was the deployment of a unifying aesthetic ideal that was manifested in the name they chose, "Greensward"—a name that can be attributed to the dear old mother England evoked by Olmsted—and the other was the influence of the landscape paintings of the Hudson by artists like Kensett. The goal was to restore in that barren territory a true fragment of the idyllic landscape of the Hudson River, to bring to the center of the city the memory of what that region had been like, to serve as an aesthetic

Aerial view of Central Park from the south by John Brachmann, 1863

and educational reference for the citizenry: in Picturesque language, it was about listening to the *genius loci*.
The proposal was a genuinely Picturesque creation evoking profound connotations of local memory and also of the European roots with which this memory and the nation could be viewed as being connected. Proposing the transformation of that barren and rocky rectilinear expanse into a naturalist

patch of countryside of Arcadian and transcendentalist inspiration was an act of audacity that excited the imagination of the jury, a symbolic gesture of reencountering an idealized vision of the local landscape.

It might be worth addressing the question of how the landscape architects of that epoch understood the notion of the *genius loci*.[5] The *genius loci* was the first point of reference for an approach to design based on attending to and studying the conditions of the site in order to establish the criteria for the intervention, not as an imposition but as a dialogue between human beings and nature, a conception that custom has now made seem "natural" but which only reached this naturalism through the implementation of Picturesque aesthetics toward the end of the eighteenth century. For the first time, a "professional" dialogue was being established with the medium of nature, in an effort to "listen." In this conception, the location takes on the role of an active entity in the process of the project, something that orients and advises, and precisely because it is endowed with a certain vitality—the *genius loci*—it permits us to establish dialogues in which the destiny of the location can be revealed to us. This is the source of the fondness for recording experience live, the passion for annotating the natural.

All of this strategic organization is undoubtedly connected with the Picturesque's interest in the duration and mobility of the aesthetic experience in relation to the "character" of the location and the architecture, admirably encapsulated in the comparative illustration from the poem *The Landscape* by Richard Payne Knight (1794),[6] where the Picturesque canon was established in opposition to the pastoral ideas of figures such as Capability Brown. Thus, if in the landscape à la Brown it is the stasis of the aesthetic experience offered by the vista that is evident, associated with the separation between architecture and garden and with the clean treatment and smoothly undulating appearance of the

5   To build, to plant, whatever you intend,
    To rear the Column, or the Arch to bend,
    To swell the Terras, or to sink the Grot;
    In all, let Nature never be forgot.
    Consult the Genius of the Place in all,
    That tells the Waters or to rise, or fall,
    Or helps th' ambitious Hill the Heav'ns to scale,
    Or scoops in circling Theatres the Vale,
    Calls in the Country, catches opening Glades,
    Joins willing Woods, and varies Shades from Shades,
    Now breaks, or now directs, th' intending Lines;
    Paints as you plant, and as you work, Designs.
Pope, A. (1731). *An epistle to the Right Honourable Richard Earl of Burlington*. Printed for L. Gilliver.
6   Knight, R. P. (1794). *The landscape, a didactic poem*. G. Nicol.

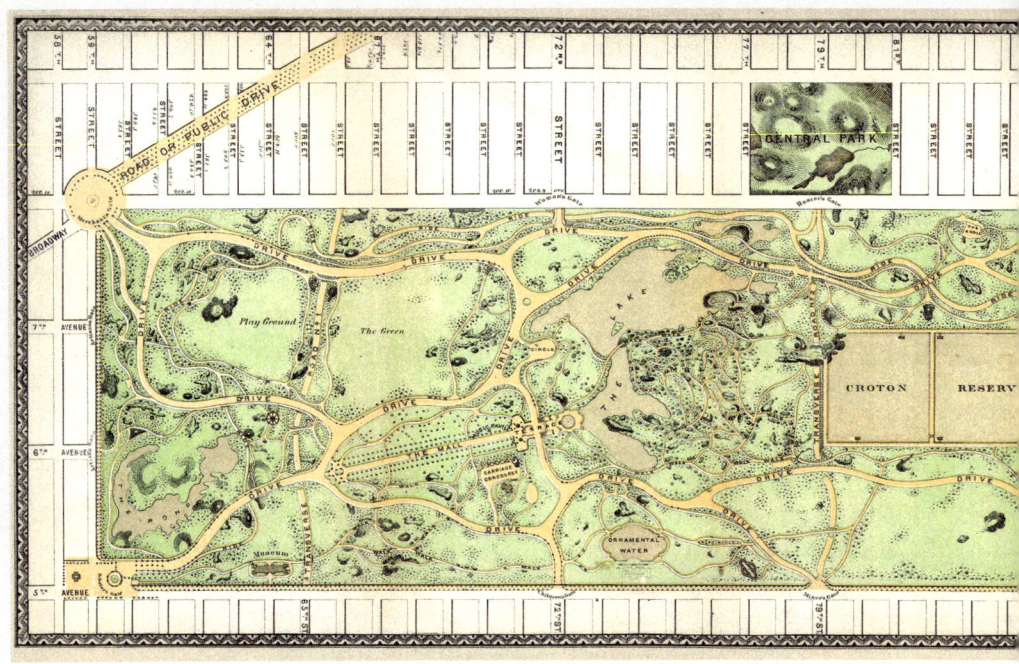

Final design of Central Park by Olmsted and Vaux

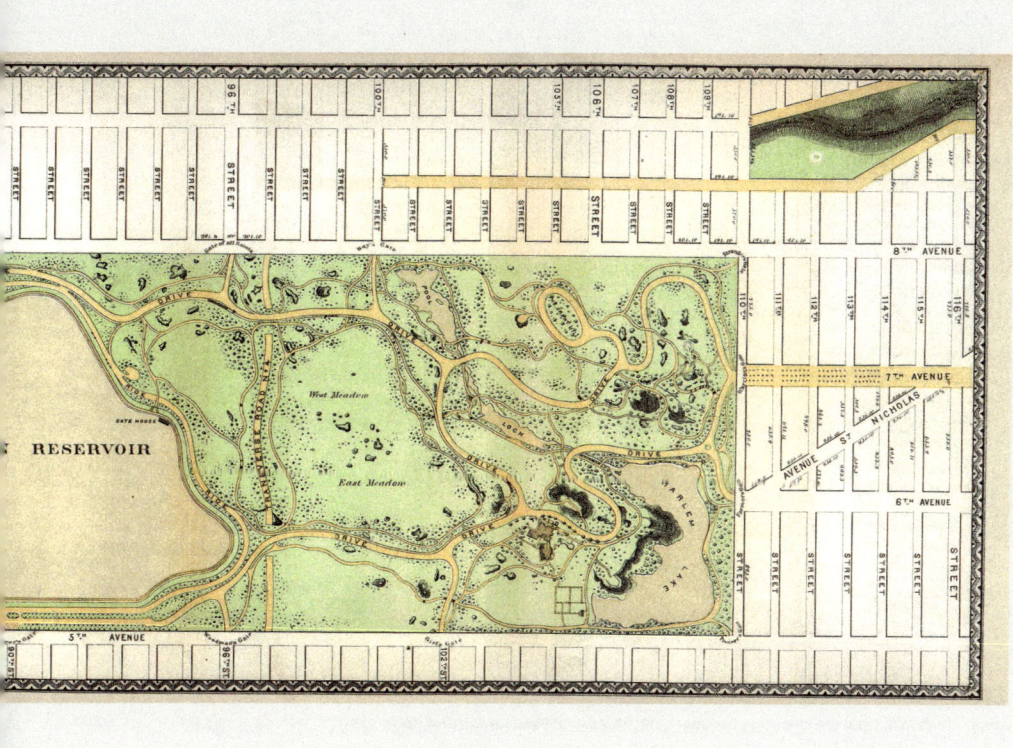

garden, in Knight's proposition, the complexity offered by nature in its most natural or wild state produces a partial concealment that arouses the curiosity and promotes the discovery of new scenes, generating a cinematic impulse in the spectator who, precisely through their curiosity and movement along winding paths, seeks out and constructs a certain narrative and sequential variety, in which the house, the path, or the bridge—artificial elements—interact with the woodlands, the hillsides, or the river in a composite totality

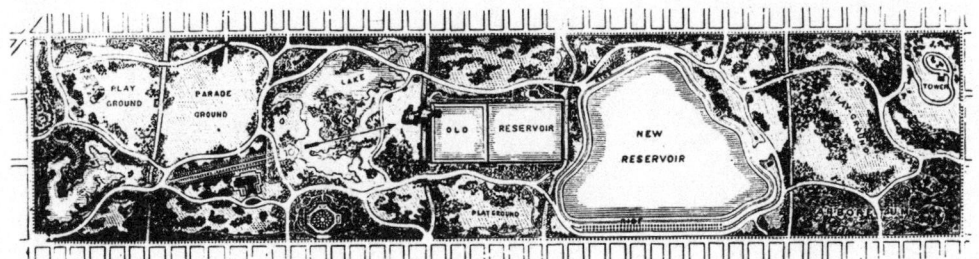

"Greensward" design from the original proposal by Olmsted and Vaux for Central Park, 1858

enveloping our experience. This dialogue was based on a correspondence of characters among natural scenes and artificial interventions which place in relief the psychologizing associations that sustain Picturesque theory, the idea that it is both these scenes and the architectural elements that, by way of their presence, transmit scale, texture, iconography, movement, etc., a particular position, or, if you like, a mood, conversing with the spectator and interacting with them. Both the house and the bridge lose their typical configuration as artificial objects in Payne Knight's depiction, and come to establish a harmony with the medium in which they are now inserted, complex and intricate, echoing the movement, continuity, and materiality of the effects produced by the Picturesque landscape, at once more complex and careless than the pastoral landscape. The analysis of Richard Payne Knight thus exhibits all of the new technical apparatus of landscape design associated with the emergence of Picturesque beauty, a genuine technical and methodological renewal that went on to also affect the way in which new scenes are valorized and aesthetically integrated, radically expanding the paltry collection of "interesting" locations handed down by the landscape tradition.

I'd like to go back over a few characteristics of the principal elements of Olmsted and Vaux's design. The Mall that they included in their proposal was guided significantly by the city grid, serving to diagonally connect the predicted main entrance from New York in the south east corner on Fifth Avenue with the visual axis of Vista Rock, as it moves away from the streets and noise of the city. From that point on and surrounding that axis, they organized the different scenes, giving priority to the appearance of expansive, rolling fields where the pre existing topography made it possible to imagine their artificial construction, and choosing to deploy the most Picturesque scenes in the locations that presented more abrupt shifts in the terrain and more Picturesque rocks, like the area to the northeast of Vista Rock, known as the Ramble, which conceals the old water tanks with underwood. Instead of demolitions, the area of the Ramble was transformed into a genuinely Picturesque scene of rocks and underwood with a frankly beautiful silhouette that was inexpensive to execute, avoiding a great deal of demolition work in this rocky area. This was all done while affording a certain priority to the southern side of the park, which had contact with the city that was then in existence, and ordered, as it were, the direction and intensity of the pathways, such that the general design of the project can be divided into two large areas, north and south: the north more picturesque and wooded, and the south more pastoral in nature and with a greater number of planned activities, with the two sections joined by the new and old reservoirs which reproduce the positioning and general form of Viele's proposition, even if the project gave more nuance to the areas on its fringes, carefully concealing them.

But the Greensward project, although clearly indebted to this methodological innovation, exhibits in its general design a patchwork development whose organizational technique calls to mind the composites of the landscape artists of the Hudson River School, in search of a range of interconnected naturalist effects that contrast with the pre existing topography and with the clearly formal parts of the program, such as the Mall or the proposed buildings. The latter are kept to a minimum, in part because they are located on the margins of the park, but also because they occupy areas that are visually isolated, in an apparent attempt—especially if we compare the proposal by Olmsted and Vaux with those of the remaining participants in the competition—to maximize the pastoral landscape, showing a sensitivity akin to that of the American landscape painters and divorced from the evocative use of ruins and architectural constructions common to the European Picturesque, pursuing what was surely an intentional strategy reinforced by the name Greensward, based on prioritizing the green spaces over other, more complex sections in order to curry favor with the jury. The positioning—in the manner of Capability Brown—of dense masses of trees on the rectilinear edges of the park completes the corrections that the project introduces to Viele's proposition and to the difficult existing conditions. The technical mastery of the creators of the project represents a qualitative leap in the use of Picturesque techniques that had hitherto principally been used on the private estates of the British aristocracy, resolving and integrating urban and topographical questions into a coherent totality capable of giving form to the public space of the new city.

The proposal was the clear winner of the contest. Neither Paxton nor Alphand submitted entries, with the total number of participants coming in at thirty-three. Nevertheless, the proposal did provoke suspicion toward, and criticism of, the optimistic expectations it projected about a terrain in which the original vegetation had been eliminated—despite the fact that the project statement made explicit mention of the drainage systems that would be necessary for success on the site—and about the appropriateness of this pastoral proposal in a context that would necessarily end up having a decidedly urban aspect. A second version had to be made which redressed a number of issues identified by the jury, such as the size of the Parade (now Sheep Meadow), which was still too large, and demanding that the winning team reorganize the traffic, separating pedestrians from horses and carriages, which positively increased the richness of the design and complexity of the park. Additionally, they decided to increase the size of the park, purchasing the land between 106th and 110th Streets, something that had been demanded multiple times since it would incorporate an area with striking topographical features, which made total sense, as it would provide the park with a kind of visual backdrop, but which Olmsted and Vaux—unlike other contestants—had prudently avoided including in their proposal so as not to lose any votes.

The combination of the bodies of knowledge that Vaux and Olmsted possessed was highly fortuitous. Both believed in the moral superiority of Picturesque aesthetics over the eclecticism of the pleasure garden and the formalism of French-inspired gardens—the other alternatives available at the time. Vaux's knowledge of landscaping and construction techniques and Olmsted's scientific approach to selecting and planting vegetation, along with their skillful use of graphic, rhetorical, and literary forms of expression had allowed them to provide a response that was at once coherent and feasible, more solid in terms of how they tailored their design to the topography, and which created an image that chimed with the social context—though from a stylistic point of view it was somewhat traditional and eclectic, as can be seen in a formal structure such as the Mall, which is incongruent with the rest of the ensemble. In fact, their eclectic mix of formalist and Picturesque landscaping techniques in the park could be seen as their principal commercial masterstroke and at the same time the greatest sign of their stylistic compromise, since they chose "and" instead of "or," that is, to please everybody, but mixed this strategy with a skill for reading the terrain, its problems and opportunities, in a truly insightful and innovative way.

This stylistic eclecticism deployed by the team then headed by Olmsted and maintained after his departure despite misgivings from some of the more orthodox members of the team, responded to a manner of understanding the design of parks which above all sought to design them as public spaces for the new democratic American city. The objective of this understanding was to place within reach of the citizenry spaces that resonated with the idealized image of nature that the culture of the time had inherited from the heyday of empiricism, with the purpose of revealing its origins in moral law, in accordance with the pedagogical ideas of transcendentalism. But in order to make this connection possible it was desirable to also introduce social areas in which the practices of conventional socialization could be fomented and accommodated, such that both individual and society would be "perfected" in a complementary fashion, offering them a sufficient and complete environmental framework that had been eliminated by the commercial city, according to Olmsted's vision.

To this end, it was necessary to conceive of the public park as an amalgam, a composite, of formal, pastoral, and Picturesque areas. There needed to be a combination of elements that were attractive to the masses and those suitable for retreat and reflection. For Olmsted, the problem was not "stylistic" but "technical": it was a matter of articulating in a coherent fashion, as a singular whole, spaces of different natures, unified by the use of living materials. And in fact, both Uvedale Price and Humphry Repton had in their day defended the fashion of including formal structures like terraces in order to establish elements of transition between the geometries of architecture and nature, showing that they were indifferent to a stylistic categorization of the forms in favor of the creation of "natural" transitions between artifice and nature. This was not a chance invention but something halfway between Price and the composite technique of the painters of the Hudson River School. Olmsted converted pre existing resources and disciplines into a method that was suited to realizing new objectives and expressive forms. If Central Park is not considered a significant milestone in the history of landscape gardening by the "experts"—indeed, in the major historical accounts, it is afforded a modest space—it is because it positioned itself from the outset as relatively detached from this tradition, even if it utilized its techniques. It is the history of the modern city and of contemporary public space in which this project inscribes itself, in a disciplinary displacement—of the discipline of landscape architects—whose repercussions in terms of how the natural environment came to be considered in urban planning traverse the entire modern arc of the twentieth century.

This aspect is also relevant because it surreptitiously introduces into landscape architecture a form of monstrosity, that of the stylistic hybrid—literally the product of crossing plants or animals of different species or genera—which contributed to the formation of new notions of beauty that only continued to grow over the course of the twentieth century.

This expansion had been announced in the texts in which Uvedale Price tackled the limits of beauty with respect to the ugly. One of the most notable original elements in his essays is his defense of deformity, negligence, and the accidental as active aesthetic categories. Price defends the Picturesque as a more open and comprehensive field than the beautiful, in which highly diverse gradations could be accommodated. As Price affirms, "deformity is to ugliness what picturesqueness is to beauty",[7] deformity and Picturesqueness are as distant from one another as the ugly and the beautiful; they share, as it were, a common ground. There is a space of negotiation between the two ideas. Thus begins a fascinating adventure in modern aesthetics that will end up divesting the traditional canons of their authority. Price gives examples of places where deformity, subject to a process of leveling, reaches the status of "Picturesque," such as in the case of mines and quarries which, being deformities, can be viewed as Picturesque spaces through minor improvements. Or the example of certain trees whose deformities caused by the wind, which are at first surprising, can come to be viewed as Picturesque if incorporated into the adequate context, making them more valuable than others which have grown in a regular fashion, precisely because of their deformity.

This nuanced consideration of deformity as something that is capable of being integrated into Picturesque aesthetics went from being received with derision to inspiring admiration when the very example of repurposing quarries as public parks saw the creation in Barón Haussman's Paris of the Parc des Buttes-Chaumont (1864–1867) under the direction of Jean-Charles Adolphe Alphand, giving form to one of the most successful and radical Picturesque manifestos, backed up by the resounding popular success of the project, which continues to this very day.

Buttes-Chaumont is possibly the best referent for the Picturesque aesthetic of the nineteenth century, the place where all the elements that have thus far been mentioned as being introduced by this vision are actively present. From its mines repurposed into public spaces we will have no trouble in understanding the vitality of the Picturesque in the arc of modernity: from Olmsted's audacity in proposing the reconstruction of an idyllic landscape typical of the

[7] Price, U. (1794). *An essay on the picturesque as compared with the sublime and the beautiful.* Hereford.

Hudson River on barren soils, which led to the creation of Central Park, through to the actions and projects of Robert Smithson to repurpose mines and open-air quarries as colossal earthworks, the Picturesque gaze unveils hidden sites, concealed by a conception of public space as a space of representation, to propose the public realm as a dialogue with nature and with the entropic contexts that demanded new cartographic practices and a new form of visibility.

Act III: The Work of Central Park and Its Urban Impact

Looking at a number of episodes in the construction of the park will help to give an outline of the type of work that the landscape architect needs to master, the combination of technical and methodological skills possessed by this new figure invented by Olmsted and inaugurated by Central Park. Landscape architects needed to be well versed in the knowledge typical of the American farmer that Olmsted had acquired during his youth. Thanks to this knowledge he understood the benefits of scientific planning and the systematic management of organic processes. Ecology—at the time a discipline still in its embryonic stages—provided Olmsted with his scientific model, a model which brought together the spheres of biology, the social, and the aesthetic, facilitating an operative methodology indebted to the "rational empiricism" of Humboldt. His move from the farm to the public space meant planning the park as a multidisciplinary project that required a team of specialists: in the case of Central Park made up of a civil engineer, an agricultural engineer, a horticulturalist, an architect, and a landscape architect. The agricultural engineer was George Waring Jr., who would propose the system of ground drainage, with a complex design and a scale that was unprecedented at the time. Olmsted and Waring—who was only twenty-four years of age—set to work on the most complex tasks, creating the necessary conditions for cultivating the plants and for managing the effects of the climate, the earthworks, and the drainage systems. To this end, they reduced the rocky areas, filling in two feet of soil, extracting the rocks and mineral matter that abounded, finishing off the pastoral areas with another two feet of plant covering, and completely flattening the area of the Mall, among other operations. William Giant was the civil engineer responsible for the design and construction of the complex and staggered network of paths designated for various forms of use. Ignaz Pilát was

A Monstrous Encounter Between Transcendentalism and Positivism

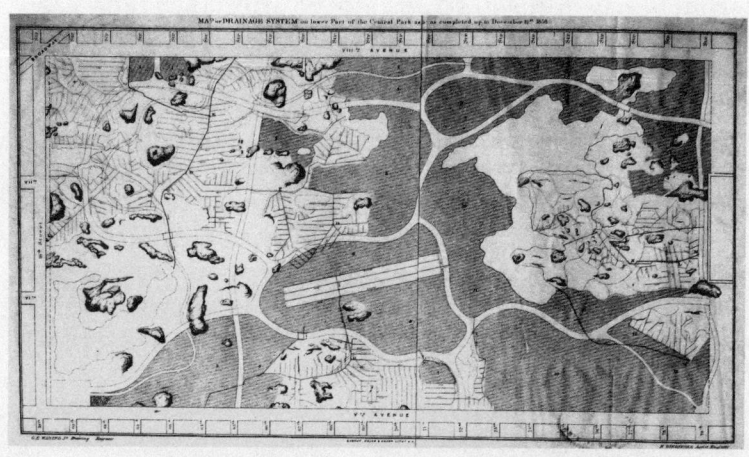

Plans and photograph of the drainage networks constructed in 1858

the horticulturalist responsible for the selection, adaptation, and maintenance of the natural materials and the specific design of the vegetation, which included the planting of 240,000 trees. They employed botanical criteria that essentially sought to reproduce the flora of the Hudson in its different ecosystems in an attempt to artificially recreate the natural sceneries promised by the Greensward project. Calvert Vaux designed the architectural structures, bridges, and more urbanized areas—such as the section formed by the Mall and the fountain at its summit—with acumen and elegance. The design, functions, and overall conception of the park fell within Olmsted's remit, though Vaux also played a role. The coordination and direction of the team, however, along with the organization and direction of the work, was Olmsted's responsibility alone, for which he acted as superintendent from 1858 to 1861. From then until 1877 he worked intermittently with the park commission—although his labor was always subject to great political tension. It was in these tasks of directing and organizing the works and management where Olmsted's reliability shone brightest, as he coordinated up to 4,000 people working simultaneously under difficult conditions—because of both financial cuts and a lack of preparation in the workforce—enabling a rapid opening of the park thanks to his almost military control of the site, based on commands handed down daily with specific instructions for the various tasks.

The public acceptance of Central Park was immediate and one of the principal reasons for the success of the profession that Olmsted launched with the park's creation. But as happens in architectural projects—in this case increased by the fragility of the natural materials—the immediate popular success often jeopardizes the stability and consolidation of the spaces and the ideas in the plan. The way the different environments were used did not always coincide with the sophisticated transcendental reasoning of Olmsted, who ended up obsessing over aspects such as indecent language or the speed at which the horses trotted. But the more important struggle that Olmsted took on was against the distortion of his original ideas both by the growing pressure to allow sports on his pastoral expanses—pressure to which he ultimately succumbed in part, designating two areas, in the north and the south, to concentrate and control these activities—and by the systematic attempt of different collectives and ethnic groups to leave their

A Monstrous Encounter Between Transcendentalism and Positivism

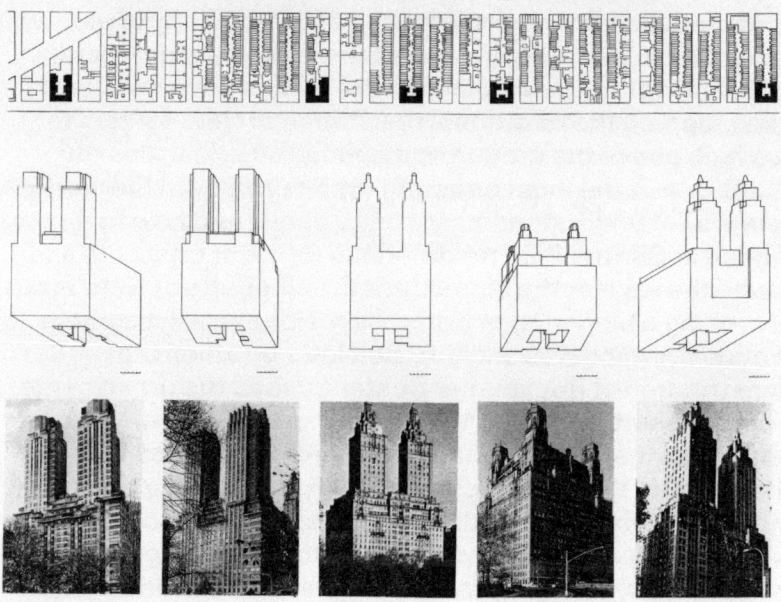

Analysis of the twin tower typology on the margins of Central Park by Joseph Fenton, taken from "The Alphabetical City", Pamphlet Architecture, no. 5, 1985

footprint on the park by way of all manner of pavilions and commemorative monuments, which Olmsted rejected as invasions that destroyed the very concept of the park, radically contradicting it.

This description of the process of the creation of Central Park and of the figure of the landscape architect cannot conclude without reference to the almost immediate urban effects to which the process led, and which meant that the undertaking was also seen as a success from the point of view of the laws of the market, creating a spatial model that lent validity to this new professional figure, since the transformative and economic impact at the urban level of his park was another virtually immediate consequence.

As such, while the residences of the great financiers quickly began to congregate in their preferred location on the east side of Central Park—along the length of Fifth Avenue between the institutions and museums—on Eighth Avenue the growing demand to live adjacent to the park led in just a short period of time to the creation of the typology of the "twin tower block," uniform high-rise blocks with the character of dual towers which, thanks to the pulling power of Central Park, toppled the traditional resistance of New Yorkers to live high above the ground and generated as early as the 1930s one of the most beautiful urban profiles in the world, a new way of understanding the metropolis and how to inhabit it. Central Park modified the forms of urban life and paved the way for the characteristic silhouette of New York, provoking a blooming of primarily residential skyscrapers around it, which was accentuated later on when the construction of Rockefeller Center pushed the urban center from Manhattan toward Midtown. The park's commercial effect was instant, and real estate agents soon realized the benefits that an investment in large public parks could induce. In this way, paradoxically, the popular success of a public space conceived as a Picturesque fragment of nature motivated by transcendentalist desires ultimately coincided with commercial laws, and this coincidence went on to become the best possible business card for the landscape architect, who could be viewed as enriching both the environment and the real estate business.

But if these effects of Central Park on the real estate market were significant, the converse effects were no less important, because the park's image and relationship with the city would go on to be positively altered as it, rapidly transformed from an isolated and artificial park surrounded by a desolate wasteland to constituting a genuine center of the vertically consolidated factory of the city, attracted by the magnetism of this void. As the woodlands grew so did the skyscrapers, creating a stark, three-dimensional presence along the rectilinear boundaries of the park. Its appearance evolved into that of a gigantic plaza or landscaped forum, and this, somewhat surprisingly—since Olmsted had always sought to erase these borders with dense tree covering—restituted the sense of it being an urban public space with which it had been conceived, in a natural and artificial process of transformation that was unprecedented at the time, a public space whose dimensions and Picturesque, almost sublime beauty continue to captivate residents and visitors alike.

The processes of constructing the modern city thus supposed a complete re-elaboration of Olmsted's concepts of landscaping owing to the growth of the park's natural materials and to the artificial limits running parallel to it: trees and skyscrapers growing together, feeding off of each other, creating a new form of Picturesque beauty that now really did envelope the city and the park in a unique whole. It is an amalgam of nature and artifice that immediately caught the imagination of the town planners and architects of Europe—and of Le Corbusier in particular—and which is the major Picturesque legacy of Olmsted, the material that we have inherited and made our own; that which our imagination has cemented as the modern public space par excellence.

Act IV: Transcendentalism Meets Positivism

On the one side we have Frederick Law Olmsted and his most emblematic work, Central Park, viewed a century after its conception through the eyes of a great contemporary photographer, Lee Friedlander (the picture is taken from the book *Viewing Olmsted*, an homage to Olmsted edited by Phyllis Lambert, consisting of three photo essays about his oeuvre created by a number of other photographers). On the other side is a hand-drawn sketch by Le Corbusier, one of his characteristic ink drawings with which he liked to illustrate his theories of the modern city, sometimes for his public lectures, in which he would draw these designs of great beauty he was talking about for the audience, and sometimes as illustrations for his numerous books. In both representations we see elements that are indisputably similar, to the point that we could think that the second is an initial sketch of a project photographed upon completion and after various decades have passed: In the foreground, vegetation that could pass for "natural," dominated by magnificent, imposing trees, framing undulating fields traversed by paths or surrounding a lake. In the background, interspersed with the branches and

Central Park, Lee Friedlander. 1991

foliage in an unarguably Picturesque manner, old constructions emerge, skyscrapers that a trained eye instantly recognizes: in the first image, those of New York, between Fifth Avenue and Fifty-Ninth Street, with the Plaza Hotel in the center; in the other, those of the City for Three Million Inhabitants, the gigantic cruciform skyscrapers that Le Corbusier began to imagine around 1920 and which, little by little, led to the notion of the "Green City."

Our gaze flits back and forth, pleased by the play of analogy and difference. It's difficult to stop looking and comparing, just as it is easy to establish threads, parallels, paradoxes, and similarities. Olmsted and Le Corbusier: two worlds that converge today but never came into contact in their times, two manners of thinking the city, from two cultures and with very different technical and ideological foundations—to simplify: transcendentalism and positivism—which, however, now seem to converge as if under a spell, not just in these pictures but also in the way in which we today conceive the modern heritage in the two of them. The American hero and the European hero, the democratic American city of the

Ville Radieuse, Le Corbusier. 1930

nineteenth century and the industrial European city of the twentieth century are synthetically represented and united in these illustrations.

Why do these phenomena gravitate toward each other from our perspective, when in their day they appeared highly divergent? 1. Because of the interest that each of the images shows in that which is complementary to its primary focus. 2. Because of the interest that each of the creators had in constructing a vision of the modern city based on the interaction between nature and artifice. 3. Because of the common link that this interest demonstrates in relating the aesthetic ideals of the eighteenth-century Picturesque with the changes in scale and methodology brought about by industrialization. 4. Because of the responsibility that both had in organizing new ways of training professionals in a number of innovative pedagogies tailored to the new disciplines of architecture and landscape architecture. 5. Because of the way in which both conceived of procedures in order to identify new ideas, with each constructing a "laboratory" of their time.

But let's return to the dual image of the thinning forest, opening up before our eyes onto a fragmentary vista of what is undoubtedly a modern metropolis with its emergent constructions emulating the vertical force of the trees that frame the scene. Olmsted's focus was placed on nature, on the idealized reconstruction of a fragment of the pastoral landscape of the Hudson River in an eroded area without woodlands, plant cover, or natural drainage. And surrounded by a city that imposed itself on the rectilinear outline of the park (in fact Olmsted masked the grid of 1811 New York with dense trees, with the intention of concealing the city and the anti-Picturesque geometry of its edges). Olmsted was determined to construct a natural space in the center of the city whose primordial function was educational, in the sense that the transcendentalists understood nature as being educational: as the place where it was revealed that the ethical and moral laws of humanity emanated from the physical laws of nature; the perfect Humboldtian harmony through which at the time it was thought that nature constituted a model in whose likeness the laws of democracy were made. It is important to realize that this represented a genuine forum, the place where the notion of the public was able to really shine. But the public had come to represent an emancipation from the natural. Both concepts, the public and nature, for Olmsted remained tied to a democratic conception of the city, as a movement that compensated for the other more impulsive and self-centered forces of capitalism.

This was all true and I'm sure it was necessary to think this way, but today we see something different. We do not value Central Park in particular for the lofty concepts that drove Olmsted to conceive of the project nor for the beauty of its design—seemingly conventional and in part unresolved— but for the harmonic way in which the trees and buildings have entered into a symbiotic union, creating an experience that is unlike any other around the world and yet somehow universal, converted into a sort of genetic code of the modern city, whether North American, Asian, Latin American, African, or in Europe. To put it pointedly: the true contemporary Picturesque vision is trees and buildings growing together, the only modality of public space in which we can move without feeling manipulated, an amalgam that we recognize and identify as "our world."

Olmsted did not know it, but he *almost* knew it: he understood and defended the mutual dependency, the mutual attraction between park and skyscraper in the metropolis, but only in an ethical way, as tendencies that mutually compensated each other. He was not able to intuit that this attraction was an attraction toward a new kind of monstrous beauty, a drastic reformulation of the Picturesque concepts to which he gave form without being able to interpret it. Unlike Robert Smithson, who much later, after his famous stroll through Central Park, named Olmsted the first "land artist." Smithson intuited with lucidity the value of this new vision, and he became Olmsted's premier critic and disciple.

Although educated in the aesthetics of the Picturesque by his teacher Charles L'Eplattenier, Le Corbusier, on the other hand, was fascinated in his youth by the brutal scale of the oommercial skyscrapers of North America at the turn of the century and the industrial technologies that made them possible, as well as by the scientific methods of construction that those technologies enabled: mass production, the assembly line, the principles of Taylorism, all that budding energy of capitalism that made it resemble a wild and contradictory force, but with a portentous beauty, which he was able to identify with an equally incontestable lucidity. He produced an image that was even more powerful than those that were coming over from the new continent: a skyscraper that replicated itself, and on an unknown scale, mass produced, Cartesian, and indifferent to all inherited conventions, each one forming a genuine city of work—which, when spaced isotropically, together compose a science-fiction landscape—an almost sublime mechanical Taylorist city: in this case, a consciously monstrous one. And a visionary one.

Le Corbusier soon counterbalanced this initial impulse with one of a very different nature: the void between the towers could not merely be passive; it was, of course, the site of motorized mobility, but it was also progressively identified as a dual space, natural and public, an immense park that was no longer confined by the borders of traditional parks, but which expanded in an undifferentiated fashion, composing a new and unique urban medium. The maximum expression of mechanization thus carried, in his head, the association of a "new primitivism." There were no parks or gardens but nature as such; the ultimate expression of industrial society integrated two ideas that until then had been antithetical and incompatible, untouched nature and mechanical skyscrapers, making them indissoluble, one and the same thing. For this reason, it is no coincidence that he adopted the designation of the "Green City" as a recurring slogan for his theories of town planning, which on the other hand understated what was most prominent and the principal object of his investigations: the skyscraper as the primary and absolute presence in the modern city.

There is a certain symmetry between Olmsted's endeavor of constructing a fragment of untouched nature within the city of skyscrapers and Le Corbusier's vision of the skyscraper as that which permits a new synthesis of the primary forces of nature and the primary forces of a mechanized society. Both notions are highly provocative, new, and original, and both were presented by their creators—both great proselytizers—as discoveries that they were generously offering to society in order to liberate it from its evils. Both facilitate an interaction—with varying degrees of consciousness—between skyscrapers and primeval nature, and both are produced by a focus on a single theme, learning its laws and modifying scales and fields of application; that is, isolating and learning to manage this theme as a new material detached from its previous realms: aristocratic in the case of the park, and speculative in the case of the skyscraper.

But we must make an observation: just as Friedlander's photograph exhibits a recomposition that we have made our own, transforming that which Olmsted imagined we would see, the image by Le Corbusier with which we are currently concerned is a small sketch with an unusual perspective that scarcely resembles the mass of representations that for years he produced in his famous, gigantic dioramas, which today are viewed as icons of Modernism. In them, the point of view was elevated above the canopy of the trees to show what was his central motif of interest: the unique splendor of the Cartesian skyscrapers in military formation, the formal triumph of industrialization, the beauty of mechanization. Time turns back on itself, even for someone as conscious of his actions and their repercussions as Le Corbusier, and thus, this magnificent sketch has come to be more widely disseminated that his demonstrative dioramas. One need only consider that this drawing is the only hand-drawn sketch included among the 700 illustrations contained in Sigfried Giedion's *Space, Time and Architecture* in order to assess its impact (something Le Corbusier could hardly have predicted, particularly since the sketch was not included in his *Complete Works*). When we experience it from below, protected by the shade of the trees and entertained by the undulation of the terrain and the paths, the Green City of Le Corbusier no longer has the appearance of a mechanized and megalomaniacal nightmare of a half-fascist and blindly positivist luminary; instead we once again feel this unique and universal experience of wandering around the interior of the genetic code of the modern city, an amalgam of nature and artifice, of architecture and public space, of city and landscape, a detailed image of an aesthetic monster that we can call the origin of a new tradition.

This leads to the paradoxical outcome where what attracts us in the image of Central Park is the skyscrapers that Olmsted never imagined would sprout with such force, and what attracts us in the image of the Green City is this forest through which we wander, divorced from the incommensurable scale of the skyscrapers which, scattered here and there, are scarcely noticed, hidden by the density of the foliage that was of little interest to Le Corbusier beyond its mere mention. This switching of the gaze between background and figure, the displacement of interest between the creators and the current audience (us), this identification of both figures with a monstrous beauty is what we could call our "legacy": what we have inherited, the relation between ancient chimeras and quotidian forms of contemporary life. This legacy, as I have already mentioned, is an amalgam, the product of the fusion in our minds of the attempts to bring about a colossal ecological restoration—an artist who worked with the magnitude of geological change is how Smithson defined Olmsted—and a technological and typological revolution of a fascistic bent, both paving the way for a topological transformation of the structure of the city that was capable of producing syntheses that had previously been unthinkable, of producing great concentrations and enormous voids that composed a unique identity. It is an interaction between nature and artifice that could never have been imagined by those authors who, in the eighteenth century, having problematized the concept of the "sublime" as being unreachable, proposed an aesthetic of the "Picturesque" that could be applied indifferently to a valley or a city, a tree or a building, a river or a highway.

Act V: Proselytism and Success

Let's forget these pictures for a moment and move on to the propaganda of aesthetic and programmatic change that both promoted. Olmsted, conceiving and founding at Harvard the first school of landscape architecture, which his son directed, wanted to train new specialists in the study of empty urban spaces and their connection to create articulated spatial systems that also exist in a dialectical relation to the "full," thus reproducing his own manner of working. The denomination of landscape architect was coined in opposition to the term "landscape gardener" inherited from Humphry Repton, because Olmsted was conscious of the fact that the essential objective of this new discipline was the construction of modern public spaces, not just nature, which was a medium to which—quite obviously, given its instrumental function—a great deal of technical attention was devoted. Following on from this step, an equally important one was made in problematizing the active presence of nature on different scales, in the city and in the countryside. If today we see national parks as possessing unarguable value, it is thanks to the great spatial and methodological apparatus created by Olmsted and his new discipline. To put it another way, to a large extent we still think of nature today as Olmsted viewed it: as a monument to protect for our pleasure and for the ethical education of coming generations; as an enormous system of natural public spaces articulated on the scale of the global city in which we live. *Monument, public space, protected*: words that betray the artificial character of "the natural," our inherited amalgam.

If we now turn to Le Corbusier, we see an endless trail of CIAM congresses, Athens Charters, and norms of all kinds, a genuine transformation of the profession promoted by way of a corporative and authoritarian format, brought about with the consensus of a small number of people, the great maestros of modernity, imposing their doctrine of pyramidal form on schools and professional organizations alike. The objective was not only to create competent

Garden on the terrace of Le Corbusier's home and studio on Rue Molinot in Paris
Studio and home of Frederick Law Olmsted in Chestnut Hill, Boston

professionals in the context of the Taylorization of society but also to renew the framework that regulated their activity (from the "Athens Charter" to the "Modulor," by way of the "Five Points," the "Seven Ways," or the "Three Human

Establishments"). But Le Corbusier's contribution is threefold: he is not just the new legislator; his mission consists in convincing people that this revolution is unavoidably necessary in an industrial context, but also that it would unleash a new form of beauty. Just like Olmsted, he thus reproduced his own creative method, transforming it into a universal pedagogical principle. If we look at his personal biography, however, we are presented with a picture at odds with the would-be positivist legislator he embodied in his youth. All of his mature works exhibit a shift toward the organic and the cosmogonic, a slow and gradual drift away from the normative and the mechanical in favor of a progressive acceptance of the "natural" condition of architecture and of those who inhabit it.

If we think about Olmsted and Le Corbusier simultaneously, the most interesting and provocative aspect is just how far our vision of them differs from their vision of themselves. We have scant interest in Olmsted as a botanist or gardener; we are interested in the organization and artificialization of the medium of nature that he brought about, the light that his work throws on the American city, his enormous capacity to transform cities—Boston, San Francisco, Buffalo, Toronto, to name just a few—and urban typologies— such as the twin residential towers that came to populate Eighth Avenue opposite Central Park. We are interested in his role as agitator with respect to the dimension of public space within capitalism and the role of nature in its construction. What is there to say about Le Corbusier? What interests us about him despite his grand legislative and Taylorist projects is his radical capacity for change, his ability to traverse all scales and to do so in a coherent though evolving fashion. We are interested in his responsibility for creating the city that we have inherited, an entropic jungle that Rem Koolhaas has dubbed the "generic city," always identical to itself and always hazy, having lost the formal precision of the figural objects, prismatic and radiant, now concealed by our perpetual movement, pollution, and the foliage of the adult trees that envelope modern spatiality right around the world.

Le Corbusier, the triumphant gardener; Olmsted, the triumphant builder, despite the men themselves and the methods we have inherited from them and in which we have been trained. In "Give Me a Laboratory and I Will Raise the World," Bruno Latour has told us what Olmsted and Le Corbusier did and how they did it, even though perhaps we have not hitherto known how to recognize it with sufficient clarity. But it was in their respective offices where they constructed their best "laboratories," and through these they modified the material practices used in the construction of the city and the landscape of the modern era.

Using the example of the identification of the anthrax vaccine by Pasteur and his famous laboratories in 1881, Latour explains that a laboratory is not a place that is detached from reality staffed by people endowed with supernatural powers, but a place with an extremely precise machinery of labor and topology. In this machinery, the first step is a movement from the world "outside," in order to isolate a phenomenon from its habitual context and to bring it into the laboratory in this new state. This is where genuine discoveries can occur, when the object of study is treated as a new "material" which, disencumbered of its exterior roles, demonstrates its vital laws in ideal conditions, its strengths and its weaknesses. By way of this knowledge of its behavior, it will become evident through trial and error how to isolate the antidote or articulate new fields of experimentation for this material.

To this end, the laboratory establishes the use of new *languages of inscription* that facilitate the study of this material, displacing traditional forms of knowledge to a new dominion and continually varying the scale of analysis, from the micro to the macro. These languages of inscription bring with them novel procedures for writing, teaching, and documenting.

The final step is a move from the laboratory to society, a movement that publicizes and promotes, in which the laboratory presents itself as the sole depository of these specialized forms of knowledge for the common good. This was the case with Pasteur, who was able to isolate the anthrax bacillus and find the laws that allowed him to isolate the antidote, something that had eluded other specialists, such as veterinarians and hygienists who were working at the level of natural reality. Presenting himself as a veritable savior of the French livestock industry, following a spectacular presentation of a trial of his vaccine, Pasteur became an undeniable social force. As Latour says: "If by politics you mean to be the spokesman of the forces you mould society with and of which you are the only credible and legitimate authority, then Pasteur is a fully political man."

The inherited city is to a large extent a hybrid product—a monstrous product, if you like—of the laboratories invented by Le Corbusier and Olmsted, of their politics. Both of

Back Bay Fens, Frederick Law Olmsted. Boston, 1892
Ministry of Health and Education in Rio de Janeiro, Le Corbusier. Brazil, 1936–1945

them isolated a phenomenon from reality, displacing it to their laboratory and converting it into a new material which, freed from the responsibilities enforced by reality, could display its full range of potentials and its fields of experimentation. Whether it was the English public park—Olmsted—or the commercial skyscrapers of America—Le Corbusier—both wrested these specimens from the hands of aristocrats or gardeners, from engineers and speculators, and transported them to their own offices. There, in isolation, they took on the appearance of a genuinely new material: modern American public space and the modern architectural type par excellence, both capable of revealing new insights and principles, a new language of inscription.

This new language is in the "five points," in the "Athens Charter," and in the "Green City" as an ideal, and it is in the texts and the appropriation of architectural techniques by Olmsted or in his way of understanding his work as consisting in coordinating bodies of knowledge and vocabularies that were previously autonomous, and thanks to him, new and confluent. Of course, both were also preceded by an outward motion: for the young Le Corbusier, his travels to the Orient and South America and the virtual presence of North America in his imagination, and for Olmsted, his journeys to the slave-holding South and to England—formative journeys in which both identified and isolated their respective objects of study.

In these laboratories, this new material is subjected to routines of trial and error, studying the potentials of its various scales, multiplying and generating systems—the center of the radiant city, the system of parks … The typology of the office and the process of working in the lab are already an anticipation of earlier pedagogical implications: the linear regulation in the manner of the assembly line on Rue de Sèvres; the imitation of the office of the American architect according to the model Olmsted had been provided by his friend H. H. Richardson in Boston. All the displacements, all the routines and movements are present. In both instances, the Latourian topological construction is present, including the final step, the educational and promotional movement from the laboratory to society: Le Corbusier and Olmsted as great educators, the true agents of the dissemination of their ideas, depicting them as urgent and necessary, the visible heads of new political visions.

Coda

I'd like to look now at two images corresponding to moments in which the maturity and recognition of their ideas is already well established. Two men, sitting with their legs crossed, contemplating expanses populated with vegetation, water, and figures that play the role of directing the gaze and the attention of the viewer: toward a bridge in the case of Olmsted and toward the figure of the Sugarloaf Mountain in the picture by Le Corbusier. We could be looking at the same individual situated in two different geographical and climatic settings. The figure of Olmsted is in the open air, contemplating an artificial creation, since not just the bridge but all of Back Bay Fens, which he is contemplating, is an artificial work of hydraulic engineering. The figure of Le Corbusier is inside a skyscraper contemplating the Picturesque forms of a tropical landscape that announces the displacement of metropolises from the cold north of the continents of the West to the tropical belt of the other continents.

Both possess an identical relationship to the medium: passive and static. They are only contemplating the landscape, entranced by the aesthetic of its Picturesque beauty. And both have a "filtered" relationship with the medium of nature. In the case of Olmsted it is because everything he is contemplating is the product of a careful process of design that allowed a piece of infrastructure such as a reservoir designed to protect against the flooding of the Charles River to take on the appearance of a natural phenomenon. In the case of Le Corbusier the landscape depicted is apparently "natural," but in the foreground we should be able to see the expansion of the city toward the beaches of Copacabana and Ipanema, which at that moment were exploiding in popularity. The position of the spectator is located in a glazed skyscraper that frames the view, forming an artificial filter in the foreground, while in the picture of Olmsted, the positions are inverted, with the bridge being singled out in the background, connecting the individual with the city. In neither image do the subjects and objects of contemplation touch or interact beyond the act of contemplation. There is a subject and an object connected by a secret hand that has activated the *genius loci* in order to shock and provoke an emotional response in the subject. Nature "poses" for him. Transcendentalism and positivism are successive and complementary components in the mechanism of the dominion of nature that runs through modernity, a period in which Bruno Latour's so insightfully named "parliament of things" has not yet been invented, reminding us that the *genius loci* has only just begun to find its voice, to face up to humans and demand an urgent dialectical and political relationship. The monster invented in modernity—and with it, us ourselves—is currently receiving new life in acquiring a fresh voice and making demands that we have globally termed "climate change," signals emitted out of its exasperation at being seen as an object of contemplation instead of an exploited, dying, and entropic interlocutor that is de calling for manding a form of attention and imagination the likes of which neither transcendentalism nor positivism could ever offer, as doomed as the creature they engendered.

Bibliography:
Burke, E. ([1756] 1990). *A philosophical enquiry into the origin of our ideas of the sublime and the beautiful*. Oxford University Press.
Collins, P. (1965). *Changing ideas in modern architecture: 1750–1950*. Faber & Faber.
Fariello, F. (1967). *Architettura dei giardini*. Edizioni dell'Ateneo.
Fenton, J. (1985). *Hybrid buildings* (Pamphlet architecture, no. 11).
Humphry, R. (1976). *The red books of Humphry Repton*. Basilisk Press.
Hussey, C. (1927). *The picturesque: Studies in a point of view*. G.P. Putnam's Sons.
Knight, R. P. (1804). *An analytical inquiry into the principles of taste*.
Olmsted, F. L. (1887). *Report of the Landscape Architect Advisory*.
Price, U. (1794). *An analytical essay on the picturesque as compared with the sublime and the beautiful*. Hereford. Extended at. (1810). *Essays on the picturesque*. Mawman, 21–22.
Rosenzweig, R. & Blackmar, E. (1992). *The park and the people*. Cornell University Press.
Walker, P. & Simo, M. L. (1994). *Invisible gardens: The search for modernism in the American landscape*. MIT Press.
Whately, T. (1770). *Observations on modern gardening*. Printed for James Williams.
Zaitzevsky, C. (1982). *Frederick Law Olmsted and the Boston park system*. Belknap Press.

Robert Smithson:
The Picturesque Entropologist

**Robert Smithson climbing a fence in a "No Trespassing" area, Great North Quarry, New Jersey, December 1966.
Photograph by Nancy Holt**

Act I: The Monuments of Passaic

Robert Smithson, who was born in 1938 in Passaic, New Jersey, and died in 1973 in Amarillo, Texas, has from the very start attracted the attention of architects and landscape architects, and for good reason. In fact, of all the artists of the seventies, aside from Gordon Matta-Clark, perhaps—who trained as an architect at Cornell—he would be the one who appropriated the broadest range of techniques and concepts from other disciplines, coining the term "earthworks," which hardly conceals the enormous debt that his work owes to Uvedale Price's and Frederick Law Olmsted's Picturesque aesthetics, but also to the architecture of the great corporations that emerged in the wake of the Second World War, from whom he would essentially go on to adopt his tools, techniques, and processes. What's more, just as Olmsted and Le Corbusier did in their day, he would create a new lexicon that enunciates in a somewhat chaotic—though highly intuitive—manner the capacity of energy and its sibling, entropy, to transform the manner of thinking the material culture of the architect, the artist, and the landscape architect. From the year 1960 until his death, Robert Smithson was, as Latour's rules of the laboratory dictate, an outstanding and tireless educator. Just like Olmsted and Le Corbusier, he sought to defend his postures as necessary and urgent, and to bring together a significant group of artists—principally from his own New York gallery, Dawn—around similar ideas, using the magazine *Artforum* as a catapult to disseminate his theories in the cultural scene of New York, and from there—as the epicenter of the art world in the seventies—to expand his work, both in terms of its scale and the technologies used and in terms of the cultural expression of his ideas and methods. But his formation as an artist was initially linked to a very Picturesque and traditional idea: that of the walk and the journey as an artistic form.

His first two trips would have distinct characteristics. One would emulate those of the Romantic landscape artists in an explicit search for the idyllic contemporary landscape, while the other would be an intellectual journey between the place and the non-place, the site and the non-site, which together with the first journey would hone his reconfiguration of landscape architecture, a century after the art of landscape painting and landscape architecture had come to take on a central role in the process of national definition that occurred in the mid-nineteenth century—something about which Robert Smithson was entirely aware. And the meaning and impact of this process would be reflected in his two final journeys, to the Great Salt Lake of Utah in 1970—where he would realize his *Spiral Jetty*—and a brief visit to

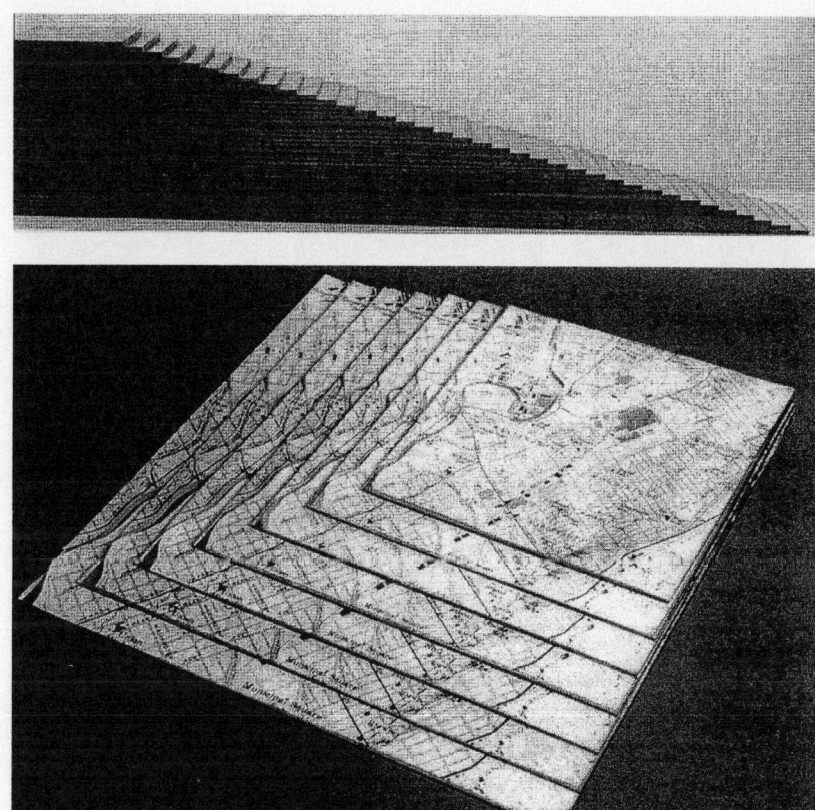

Robert Smithson, *Glass Stratum*, 1967, glass, 45 × 30.5 × 274 cm
Robert Smithson, *Untitled (Map on Mirror-Passaic, New Jersey)*, 1967, mirrors, 35.5 × 35.5 × 2.1 cm

the Whitney Museum followed by a walk through Central Park in New York in 1973, in an important reencounter with Olmsted, reflected in his final written work, which could therefore be read as a genuine artistic testament. He would die in a plane crash in 1973, the year of the first major oil crisis, which would turn Smithson into a visionary figure or shaman of a new culture.

Robert Smithson, *The Monuments of Passaic*, 1967, black-and-white prints from the original negatives, 7.5 × 7.5 cm

The perception of nature as an aesthetic experience played a central role in his formative years, and he showed signs of a precocious interest in botany and art. His mentor, the poet William Carlos Williams, author of the epic poem *Paterson*[1] (1946–1958)—one of the high points of American poetry, in which the narration of the life of the author becomes indistinguishable from the description of the course of a river (the Passaic) and from the changes in the city in which he lives, in a genuine amalgamation of subject, nature, and artifice—undoubtedly left a mark on the young Smithson, who for his first artistic or Picturesque walk chose this very mythic place in the cultural geography of America, his native city, which by then had become a depressing suburb of New Jersey.

His education was also influenced by his numerous visits during childhood to the Museum of Natural History in New York, where he admired the dioramas recreating various natural habitats and the osteological reconstructions of prehistoric animals. Soon, in the early sixties, his contacts with the New York cultural scene, Beat Generation writers, and artists who would form the core of the Minimalism and Land Art movements would bring him to initiate a process of maturation that would oscillate between biomorphic, pictorial compositions inspired by Pop Art, and Minimalist sculptures based on geomorphological laws, with a totemic use of industrial glass, whose application in elemental figures calls to mind stratigraphic cross-sections. But at the same time, together with a number of his friends from the art scene, he began to develop an interest in "low-profile landscapes," frequenting quarries, industrial wastelands, and run-down regions of suburbia. This is the origin of his expedition to Passaic, which he undertook in September of 1967, leaving from Penn Station in New York on a bus, armed with a small camera.

Despite having all the appearance of a typical Sunday outing, this trip would lead to the revelation of a new plein air program. It would culminate in an article published that same year in *Artforum*—"The Monuments of Passaic: Has Passaic replaced Rome as The Eternal City?"[2]—in which he narrates his "adventure," which is not in search of a primeval and inaccessible nature or a site marked by the presence of architectural constructions and historical ruins, as we might

1 Williams, W. C. (1948). *Paterson*. New Directions.
2 Smithson, R. (1967). "The monuments of Passaic". *Artforum*, 6(4), 48.

expect of Romantic travelers, but a suburban landscape eroded by the construction of a highway and by various forms of industrial waste. On this walk through the outskirts of his hometown he would encounter and photograph the fortuitous forms of a "new monumentalism." Javier Maderuelo has described this journey as follows:

> Smithson proposes an inversion of the Romantic sensibility, contemplating the industrial installations as ruins which, with the passing of time, could be immortalized by history. In order to attain this vision, he contemplates the locations through a distanced eye afforded him by the lens of the camera. This distance helps to give an ambience of unreality to things that are all too familiar. Thus, for example, a group of six heavy pipes spewing industrial residue into the river is photographed by Smithson and titled "The Fountain Monument," observing it as if it were the Trevi Fountain. For him, the monuments are not, therefore, heroic tributes in the traditional sense. Just like the Colosseum, the Roman Forum, or the Castel Sant'Angelo found in Rome have come to be monuments, Smithson qualifies as monuments these elements that were not erected in order to terrify or mythologize; these constructions are anti-monuments, tributes to the suburbs, memories of an exhausted, undone, and entropic industrial landscape. They are insignificant monuments which, observed as if they were heroic landscapes from other epochs, have come to be conceived as sublime. This article by Robert Smithson from the year 1967 announces a shift in sensibility that points to the recuperation of the aesthetic categories of the sublime and the Picturesque articulated in the middle of the eighteenth century by way of the recuperation of a certain type of perspective on the landscape.[3]

This may be the most relevant feature of the trip to Passaic. Smithson constructs and documents a reality that he confronts as if it were that of Williams's poem *Paterson*, with an almost comic stubbornness, reminiscent of the humor

3   Maderuelo, J. (2012). *Caminos de la escultura contemporánea* (Vol. 13). Ediciones Universidad de Salamanca.

of Buster Keaton, discovering a new Picturesque position that emerges from the acceptance of the world inherited from modernity. For Smithson, in its accidents and negligence, in its capacity to evoke what was and is, the hand of nature and the hand of man, this soulless post industrial landscape has a strange beauty, similar to that which Uvedale Price perceived in the quarries or in a tree ripped open by lightning. From this perspective, Smithson will introduce into the universe of landscape architecture a new vein of territories that he will dub "entropic sites"; a vast collection of places marked by the erosive impact of modern industries that have been condemned to the realm of the invisible. Smithson looks at modernity as if it were a force of nature and understands that its invisible places can—and must—acquire a visibility that is equivalent to that which Picturesque aesthetics endowed upon wild and entangled places, or those that are deformed by the action of nature and humanity. The deformity introduced by the machine is likewise capable of acquiring beauty if the gaze makes the effort to view it beyond the present as a sign of invisible processes. Smithson is already located on the other side of modernity, and sees entropy as something fascinating because of its capacity to leave indelible traces on a terrain—marks that exhibit all the evocative power of a colossal ruin.

It is relevant to sketch out the construction of the perspective that Smithson develops, its fixation on a specific angle, focused toward the ground, hardly leaving any space for the horizon, allowing itself to be carried away by the almost infantile attraction produced by the conglomerations of nature and industrial detritus. Right from the start, Smithson's gaze is directed at the ground, moved by certain material qualities that he intuits have not been explored sculpturally. In this way, he discovers not just other kinds of places but an amalgam of earth and various other living, inert, and artificial materials, which motivates him to move beyond the vertical canvas with the horizon as a guide, but on the plane of the ground, working with its own materiality. In his 1968 expedition to Oberhausen in Germany, accompanied by Bernard and Hilla Becher, the distance between their photographs and his becomes evident. The Bechers, fascinated by the force of the industrial constructions present here, produce their characteristic "portraits" of obsolete industries from an eye-level perspective; Smithson, literally stuck to the ground, fascinated by the marks of the industrial processes on the soil, gathers textures and traces. Smithson is not the only person to be transfixed by these desolate industrial landscapes, which were capable of rousing evocations of protohistoric times. Just a few years earlier, between 1964 and 1966, the English architect Cedric Price (1934–2003) had fixed his gaze on North Staffordshire, in his own words an arid and dirty place, rough industrial country, a region occupied by abandoned pottery factories surrounded by discarded materials and a complete railway

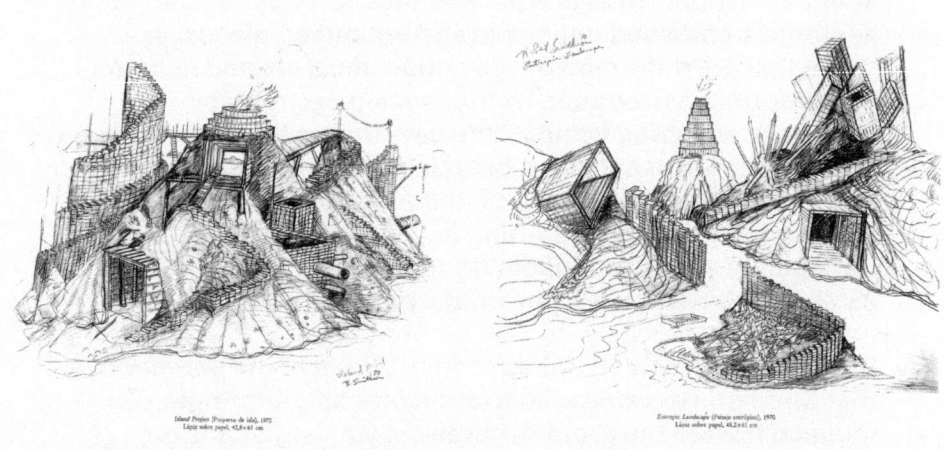

Robert Smithson, *Island Project*, 1970, pencil on paper, 42.8 × 61 cm
Robert Smithson, *Entropic Landscape*, pencil on paper, 1970, 42.8 × 61 cm

infrastructure—a place where Price grew up, like Smithson did in Passaic, and in which his family had founded a factory in the early eighteenth century. The attraction to this region in ruins drove him to conceive of a visionary project, the Potteries Thinkbelt, which renewed this industrial landscape, transforming it into a piece of university infrastructure. Maintaining the status quo of the place— its *genius loci*, we might say—he imbued it with vitality, adding a number of new constructions to form an amalgam with the industrial ruins of genuinely Picturesque inspiration; "battlefields of the Industrial Revolution," as Stanley Matthews calls them. With a perspective bearing great similarities to that of Smithson, we could say that Cedric Price is to a certain extent an architectural alter-ego of Robert Smithson.

Contemplating the new "landscape of knowledge" that Cedric Price proposes, we cannot avoid seeing reflections of all the Smithsonian themes: the erosion, the accumulation of detritus forming deposits of material and the movement and the sound of the dilapidated machinery, desolation as a framework that is gentle enough to allow the unfolding of a

Potteries Thinkbelt, Staffordshire, United Kingdom. Cedric Price, photomontages of the unbuilt project, 1964–1966

new culture—to a certain extent viewed as the sole framework that would afford a new innocence. And also—why not come right out and say it—there is something infantile in this attraction to detritus, to trains, to recycling and bricolage, to junk and waste. This materiality and these sites and techniques would go on to constitute the nucleus of the revitalization of the ideas of Picturesque aesthetics. Robert Hobbs defines Smithson as "the great rediscoverer of the Picturesque; he looked for ways to understand devastated industrial areas, to take hold of them in aesthetic terms, and he found a ready-made concept in the Picturesque, which deals primarily with change, and which assumes an aesthetic distance between viewer and landscape."[4] "Change" and "aesthetic distance" are spatiotemporal coordinates that describe Smithson's themes and for which the artist himself found a definition that was even more synthetic, borrowing a neologism proposed by Claude Lévi-Strauss: the "entropologist."

Act II: The Entropologist

For Smithson, there is a profound harmony between human action and the processes of nature, and this harmony provokes an immediate expansion of our magnitudes of time, from geological processes to industrial ones, whose "revelation" he saw as one of the central tasks of artistic activity. In his text about Passaic, he summed it up succinctly: "I am convinced that the future is lost somewhere in the dumps of the non-historical past."[5]

Scarcely a year after publishing his text on Passaic in *Artforum*, he insisted on the significance of time as a sculptural instrument: "the 'present' cannot support the cultures of Europe, or even the archaic or primitive civilizations; it must instead explore the pre- and post-historic mind; it must go into the places where remote futures meet remote pasts."[6]

Smithson was certainly familiar with the texts of Uvedale Price, whom he cited continually, and from whom he had learned just how inherent the theme of time was to the appearance of the Picturesque aesthetic, both in terms of the experience of the spectators—who abandon their contemplative stasis in order to organize the choreographic succession of the scenes by way of their mobility—and the special emphasis Uvedale Price placed on seeing the traces of the passing of time and of negligence and abandonment in untouched nature as something endowed with an enormous evocative force.

Smithson was also familiar with the texts of the anthropologist Claude Lévi-Strauss (1908–2009), who provided his innovative plein air vocation with an intellectual framework equivalent to the theories of Humboldt for Olmsted, or

4   Hobbs, R. & Smithson, R. (1981). *Robert Smithson, sculpture*. Cornell University Press, 29.
5   Smithson, R. (1967). "The monuments of Passaic." *Artforum*, 6(4), 26.
6   Smithson R., exhibition catalogue (1993). *Una sedimentación de la mente: proyectos de la tierra*. IVAM, 125–132. Originally published as "A sedimentarion of mind: Earth projects." *Artforum*, 7.

those of Nietzsche for Le Corbusier and Bruno Taut. In *The Savage Mind*[7] (1962), Lévi-Strauss had proposed the transposition of the term "entropy" to the sphere of human societies, in an effort to reflect his finding that the more complex the cultural organization of a society, the more

Robert Smithson, *Asphalt Lump*, 1969, asphalt, 20 × 90 × 66 cm

developed its structure, the closer it moves to a state of disintegration, the more "entropy" it produces. This idea enabled him to distinguish between evolved, "hot" societies, which produce waste, and others, so-called primitive or "cold" societies, conceiving the role of the anthropologist as

7   Lévi-Strauss, C. (1962). *La pensée sauvage*. English edition (1966). *The savage mind*. Weidenfeld & Nicolson.

that of an expert in social entropy, an "entropologist," to quote the author. When Smithson adopted this neologism, entropologist, he also embraced the position of Lévi-Strauss, who, through his dedication to the study of human behavior in "primitive" societies, where the relationship with nature is closest, offers Smithson a model of thought that is no longer centered—like that of Humboldt or Darwin—around the natural order but around the participation of cultural processes in a greater biological order. *Tristes Tropiques*,[8] which Lévi-Strauss published in 1955 and Smithson consulted time and again, is a special kind of travelogue that seeks to reflect upon the very meaning of the anthropological journey—which is also a journey through time, on the one hand seeking to study the origins of humanity, on the other aiming to explain the structure of "hot" societies. In this book, Lévi-Strauss recreates his anthropological passion, which is tinged with a profound nostalgia for the innocence of origins, motivated by his awareness that he is observing the final stages of the world he is studying, which is no longer isolated from "civilization," in part due to his own presence. Smithson would come to understand the mission of the artist in a world that is no longer natural, a mission that is analogous to that which Lévi-Strauss imagines for himself: to identify the past within the present, to restore a gaze that is capable of seeing presences and absences at the same time, and to establish a relationship between this amalgam of sterile countryside and industrial wasteland— which is definitively the physical medium of the postindustrial era and has extended right across the planet— and the phenomenon of life in its most original expression.

In the same manner as the anthropologist approaches identifying patterns of social conduct, the role of the artist conceived by Smithson is not to issue value judgments, but to create their own field of observation, learning to look at it and interact with it, attempting to understand and find its structures and patterns: "to organize this mess of corrosion into patterns, grids, and subdivisions is an aesthetic process that has scarcely been touched."[9] Smithson does not allow himself to be trapped by the moralist discourse of the ecologists. Certainly he conceived of his oeuvre as a work of "denunciation." His area, his field, is entropy considered in aesthetic terms in the light of the original theories of the Picturesque. For him, there is as much fascination in the

8   Lévi-Strauss, C. (1963). *Tristes tropiques*. Atheneum.
9   Smithson R., exhibition catalogue (1993). *Una sedimentación de la mente: proyectos de la tierra*. IVAM, 125–132. Originally published as "A sedimentarion of mind: Earth projects." *Artforum*, 7.

entropic processes of remote eras as in the transformative capacity of modernity; in his imagination, they are one and the same thing: "processes of heavy construction have a devastating kind of primordial grandeur."[10] He situates himself between two poles, the industrial and the ecological. The entropologist is an expert in natural and human entropies, in relating them to one another, making the implicit dialectic in erosive processes flourish. "Art can become a resource, that mediates between the ecologist and the industrialist. Ecology and industry are not one-way streets, rather they should be crossroads. Art can help to provide the needed dialectic between them."[11] Consequently and unsuccessfully, Smithson would offer his services to multiple companies with mines and open-cut quarries, proposing to transform the impact of their work on the landscape into forms of sculptural expression.

This interest in mediating between ecologists and industrialists takes us to another date that has been underlined with typical Swiss precision by Philip Ursprung: the day of June 17, 1966, when Walter Prokotsch, architect and partner at the office of Tippets, Abbett, McCarthy & Stratton, attended a talk given by Smithson at Yale University under the title "Shaping the Environment: The Artist and the City," as a consequence of which Prokotsch invited Smithson to act as a collaborating artist on the terminal that his office was developing for Dallas/Fort Worth Airport. Over the ensuing months, Smithson familiarized himself with the design techniques of architecture: "the 28-year-old artist encounters architectural sketches and terminology, grids, infrastructure, aerial photographs, and various media employed in planning mega-structures, significantly broadening his horizons."[12] Although this collaboration did not prosper, with the project being transferred to another company in June of 1967, Prokotsch's invitation marked the starting point of the growth of an art form that usurped the methodological apparatus of the architect, allowing Smithson—along with his dialectical invention of the site/non-site—to develop pieces on huge scales, bringing to the gallery documentation of his activities in the form of films, photos, scale models, soil samples, and the like. This work was supported financially by Virginia Dawn, director of the Dawn Gallery, which acted as a "client," buying plots of land that

[10] Smithson, R. Untitled, 1971, in Smithson, R. & Holt, N. (1979). *The writings of Robert Smithson: essays with illustrations*. New York University Press, 220.
[11] Ibid.
[12] Ursprung, P. *Architecture under pressure: The legacy of earth art*. at Forster, K. (2004). *Focus*. Fondazione La Biennale di Venezia, 150–163.

were abandoned or of interest to Smithson, or to the group of artists represented by the gallery.

Thus, his work adopted architectural techniques, methods, scales, and materials, a genuine professional "intrusion," as

Robert Smithson, *Spiral Jetty*, Great Salt Lake, Utah, April 1970

Philip Ursprung has remarked, which reminds us of a similar monstrous condition that we have seen at other times and at the hands of other figures we have cited in this book. This proximity to the methodological practices of the architect is not limited to manipulating entropic sites; it also contains an explicit architectural proposal to revise the spaces of the culture, as some of Smithson's sketches show, especially those that seek to construct entropic environments on new sites, realized with landfill combined with tunnels, wells, footbridges, and containers, composing amalgams of detritus that often form "building-islands," pieces that serve an exemplary function of creating a new prototype halfway between an earthwork and a museum of natural sciences for an entropic age. Inspired by the engravings of Piranesi's *Prisons*, he imagined these proposals as museums that could remain empty and exhibit themselves—as he often proposed—so as to make illegible within them all traditional disciplinary divisions …

Act III: *Spiral Jetty* and Central Park

Without a doubt the most complete example of an earthwork—at once an act of landscape architecture and a proposal for a museum, site, and non-site—is his *Spiral Jetty* at Rozel Point. A product of Smithson's trip to the Great Salt Lake of Utah, the first of the journeys that bring this trajectory to a close—journeys that were already conclusive, "mature," if you like, despite how paradoxical this distinction seems given that barely a few years had passed since his trip to Passaic—*Spiral Jetty* is an earthwork of some 480 meters in length, constructed in April of 1970 when he was thirty-two years old, which is today owned by the Dia Art Foundation and re-emerging from the lake after years lying hidden by the level of the water. The intervention was accompanied at the non-site of Dawn Gallery by a well-known descriptive text, a series of preparatory drawings, a beautiful film, and a photograph. With this work—both the one he executed in Utah and the documents presented in New York—Smithson unveiled a complete transdisciplinary methodology and a genuine contemporary observatory in which we can evaluate both his debt to Picturesque ideas and his contribution to their cultural adaptation and expansion.

His interest in salt lakes was connected to the reddish colorization characteristic of the activity of the bacteria that live in the salt pans, demonstrating the chemical proximity of blood and primordial seas. Documenting these themes, he came across a local indigenous legend that described the lake as being connected to the ocean via a tunnel created when the continents separated. This image, which for Smithson merges with the crystalline helicoid structures in the salt, restored in his imagination geological time and its formal structures, leading him to work on diagrams and drawings with the pattern of the spiral. He imagined a construction of a significant size beginning on the banks and extending into the lake, materializing the deep structure of the site, which in his imagination unified the present and the atavistic: a jetty that connects with primordial cosmic forces—which he himself described as an "immobile cyclone"—created from the inert materials that surround the lake, dried-out mud and basalt, churned up by dump trucks

Robert Smithson building *Spiral Jetty* (1970), Great Salt Lake, Utah, April 1, 1970. Photograph by Gianfranco Gorgoni

and excavators, which Smithson associated with dinosaurs, due to their size, voracity, and physical similarities. He chose to build it where some recent rusty ruins imbued the site with signs of human activity, giving "evidence of a succession of man-made systems mired in abandoned hopes."[13] In this setting, he also found an explicit reference to landscape painting: "there was Van Gogh with his easel on some sun-baked lagoon painting ferns of the Carboniferous Period."[14] The construction of the jetty was documented in a 16 mm film that records three stages of the work: the approach to

13 Smithson, R. (1972). *The Spiral Jetty*. Arts of the environment.
14 Ibid.

the site, both physically and intellectually, in which various geological, archaeological, and biological data mentioned are superimposed over shots closing in on the scene; the construction of the jetty, alternating between brief shots of the machinery in action and the mass of rocks and mud, with close-ups of the water and the crystalline forms of the salt; and a long final sequence of extraordinary beauty in which the artist himself walks along his work, filmed from a helicopter, which links his movement with wide shots of the jetty and the lake, seeking to trap the reflections of the rays of the setting sun in the center of the lake. A still image of the artist's studio with a photograph of the jetty on the wall, a light bulb hanging from the ceiling, and the film rewinding in the projector concludes the film. In a montage in which there are frequent intrusions of cartography and images of prehistoric animals taken in the National Museum of Natural History in New York, the voice of Smithson narrating his experiences lends continuity to a sound track in which there is a constant alternation between the almost complete silence of nature and the noisy industrial sounds of the various machines that punctuate the action: a truck in the first part, dumpers and excavators in the second, and the helicopter in the third.

In its double existence, both real and filmed, *Spiral Jetty* offers us a complete representation of the Smithsonian method: the tour, the journey understood as a process of approach and discovery, as an interior journey—the artist himself encoiled in the centripetal force of the jetty—and as a physical and spiritual elevation that uses the mirrored surface of the lake and the reflection of the sun to give depth and a cosmic dimension to the work. As such, it constructs a gaze that valorizes a site that would seem to be dead and devoid of "landscape" qualities.

An image gradually emerges of the artist as entropologist, architect, and landscape architect, a true monster with four heads. The mission of the artist is to reveal the temporality of natural, historical, and biological processes; a demiurge who catalyzes the distinct forces of nature and history, capable of bringing together geological magnitudes of time and cosmic spaces, of establishing and offering a dialogue that intensifies and expands the limits of experience. In Smithson, place takes on a new public dimension, derived from the understanding of his action as the construction of a true observatory that seeks to reveal the temporal structure of natural phenomena. He works with the affinity between natural and artificial entropic processes, his actions located—as he himself says—between the industrialist and the ecologist, establishing a relation between the transformative forces of humanity and the natural forces that have left their imprint on the place. The four natural materials of the site—mud, salt crystals, rocks, and water, as Smithson recites in his refrain—are manipulated by way of an instrumental technique that is genuinely industrial

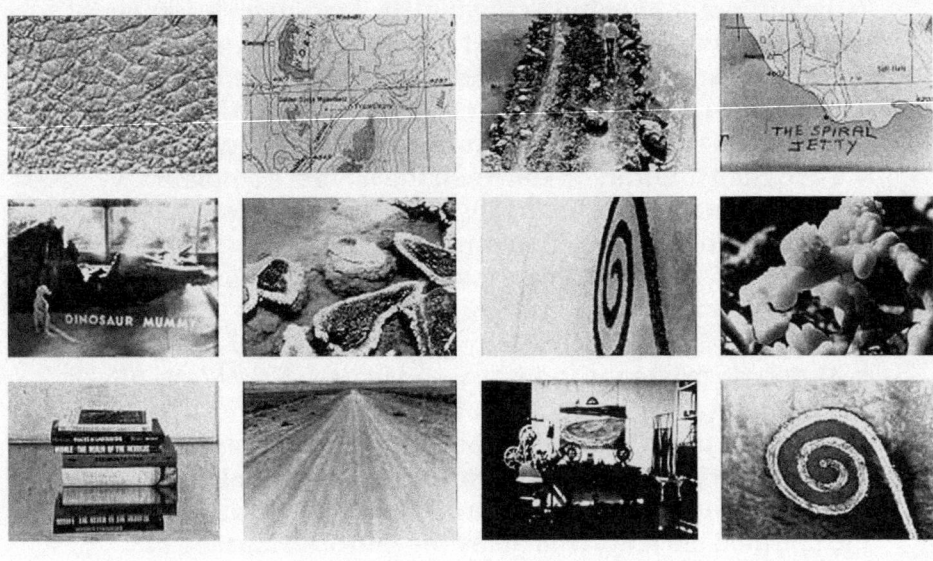

Robert Smithson, stills from the 16 mm film *The Spiral Jetty*, 1970

and artificial, including its own filming, which gives an account of the intervention, making its original meaning explicit.

Thus, the form of the spiral emerges by way of different substrates:

- Geological dimension: the origin of the lake in the movement of tectonic plates. Construction with the materials produced by the natural entropic processes.

- Archeological dimension: diverse prehistoric and historic remnants. Interpretation of the site by its indigenous inhabitants as the center of the world, a hole that connects with the "other side." Physical resemblance between prehistoric reptiles and the machinery used.

- Biological dimension: salt with its helicoid molecular structure. Red coloration of the lake identifying the origin of blood and water.

- Cosmological dimension: helicoid stellar formations (Milky Way). Reflection of the sun on the water giving three-dimensional form to a construction made of earth and observed from the air, the four elements activated in the construction of the observatory.

There is also, without a doubt, a mythical or sacred dimension, which Smithson does not shy away from, based on the association of the sun in multiple cultures with a divinity and its representation in the form of a helix. The helix is present not just in the form of the jetty but also in the movement of Smithson traversing the work, in the spinning blades of the helicopter, and in the shape of the film as it rewinds in the editing room, the final image of the recording, creating a connection between the site and the non-site, underlining the active role of the filming in the whole ensemble, as a resource for the mental journey it proposes to the viewer.

The sun is mentioned recurrently as a totalizing presence at the site—"the shore of the lake became the edge of the sun, a boiling curve, an explosion rising into a fiery prominence"; "swirling within the incandescence of solar energy were sprays of blood,"[15] and so on—lending it a catalyzing role in the creative process, which allows us to view all the action as the construction of a solar observatory, something that becomes visible at the conclusion of the filming.

Spiral Jetty represents the culmination of a way of understanding creative processes and the landscape that is as innovative as the vision of Frederick Law Olmsted was in his day. And it is Olmsted himself who is the protagonist of Smithson's final journey, an insignificant stroll in spatial terms—leaving his studio in New York to see the exhibition on Olmsted and Central Park at the Whitney Museum, followed by a little walk through the park, a few blocks away from the museum—but with a great symbolic dimension,

15 Smithson, R. (1972). *The Spiral Jetty*. Arts of the environment.

as Smithson uses it to establish a relation between his ideas and those of Olmsted, proceeding to establish a complete genealogy of the Picturesque in crowning Olmsted the first "earthwork artist."

One relevant aspect of this walk and the ensuing texts is that for Smithson, Olmsted is not a "modern" artist but a "contemporary" one, a pioneer of a new entropic landscape art. And he is, in the sense that his vision of the Picturesque opens up a totalizing understanding of natural and human actions. Smithson would use his text about Olmsted to attack the one-dimensional vision of scientistic (ecological) tendencies of the time, citing the paragraph about the quarry in Uvedale Price, to which I referred earlier:

> Some of our present-day ecologists, who still see nature through eyes conditioned by a one-sided idealism, should consider the following quote from Price.
>
> The side of a smooth green hill, torn by floods, may at first very properly be called deformed, and on the same principle, though not with the same impression, as a gash on a living animal. When a rawness of such a gash in the ground is softened, and in part concealed and ornamented by the effects of time, and the progress of vegetation, deformity, by this usual process, is converted into picturesqueness; and this is the case with quarries, gravel pits, etc., which at first are deformities, and which in their most picturesque state, are often considered as such by a levelling improver.[16]

Olmsted would have known how to integrate this notion of the Picturesque into Central Park precisely because, like Smithson, he had projected a comprehensive perspective of the geological temporality of the site, reading the effects of the ice ages and the tectonic plates on the topography, and the effects of human action in the form of deforestation, as active and disruptive materials in his Greensward proposal. To bring it to fruition, though, he had deployed a dialectical concept—not a formalist and static one—of the Picturesque, which included the process of construction

---

16 Olmsted, F. L. (1810). *Three essays on the picturesque*, quoted in Smithson, R. (1973). "Frederick Law Olmsted and the dialectical landscape." *Artforum*, 11(6).

and social demands: "Price, Gilpin, and Olmsted are forerunners of a dialectical materialism applied to the physical landscape. Dialectics of this type are a way of seeing things in a manifold of relations, not as isolated objects. [...] Olmsted's parks exist before they are finished, which means in fact they are never finished; they remain carriers of the unexpected and of contradiction on all levels of human activity, be it social, political, or natural."[17] For Smithson, Olmsted had adopted the position of the entropologist when

Robert Smithson, *Stair Rocks* (1972). Photograph by Robert Smithson of an area called "The Ramble" in Central Park, New York

he sought to renew the terrain of Central Park, functioning as a geological agent caught between contradictory forces. Smithson was also fascinated by the use of technical resources—such as installing drainage and leveling the site—that the construction of this earthwork had implied, which were similar to those of his own works, and which he understood as part of the artistic process that Central Park came to be in his imagination. In the text that he wrote about his visit, the Picturesque in Olmsted is the older sibling of Smithson's entropologist.

17 Smithson, R. (1973). "Frederick Law Olmsted and the dialectical landscape." *Artforum*, 11(6).

The exhibition on Olmsted at the Whitney Museum of American Art could not have been more opportune in Smithson's eyes, since in the dialectic between the exhibition and the reality of Central Park, the dialectic between the site and the non-site materialized, which honed his vision of his artistic practices. For him, the "maps, photographs, and documents in catalogue form [...] are as much a part of Olmsted's art as the art itself."[18] This vision is surely not so far removed from the way Olmsted might have viewed his work, as is demonstrated by the central role that he always afforded—just like Smithson—the presentation of his proposals, whether the written word or the photographic documentation of the process of construction. For Smithson, it is in the terrain of art that Olmsted can be interpreted: "The magnitude of geological change is still with us, just as it was millions of years ago. Olmsted, a great artist who contended with such magnitudes, sets an example which throws a whole new light on the nature of American art."[19]

Bibliography:
Flam, J. & Smithson, R. (1996). *Robert Smithson: The collected writings*. University of California Press.
Hobbs, R. & Smithson, R. (1981). *Robert Smithson: Sculpture*. Cornell University Press.
Hobbs, R. & Smithson, R. (1982). *Robert Smithson: A retrospective view*. Herbert F. Johnson Museum of Art.
Price, C. & Hardingham, S. (2016). *Cedric Price works 1952–2003*. Architectural Association.
Robert Smithson exhibition catalogue. (1993). IVAM.
Roberts, J. L. & Smithson, R. (2004). *Mirror-travels*. Yale University Press.
Shapiro, G. (1995). *Earthwards: Robert Smithson and art after Babel*. University of California Press.
Smithson, R. & Holt, N. (1979). *The writings of Robert Smithson: Essays with illustrations*. New York University Press.
Tsai, E., Butler, C. H., Crow, T. E., Alberro, A., Roth, M., Smithson, R., & Museum of Contemporary Art. (2004). *Robert Smithson*. Museum of Contemporary Art; University of California Press.

18 Smithson, R. (1973). "Frederick Law Olmsted and the dialectical landscape." *Artforum*, 11(6).
19 Ibid.

Robert Smithson: The Picturesque Entropologist

Three Delirious Skyscrapers[1]

Bruno Taut, *Alpine Architecture*, illustration 8, "Grotesque Region with Wrought Summits"

[1] Three Delirious Skyscrapers was presented as a lecture on March 31, 2020, as part of the Master's in Advanced Architectural Projects (MPAA11) at the ETSAM (Universidad Politécnica de Madrid).

And do you know what "the world" is to me? Shall I show it to you in my mirror? This world: a monster of energy, without beginning or end; a firm magnitude of force that does not get bigger or smaller, that does not expend itself but only transforms itself; a whole, of unalterable size, a household without expenses or losses, but likewise without increase or income; enclosed by "nothingness" as a boundary; not something blurry or wasted, not something endlessly extended, but set in a definite space as a definite force, and not a space that might be "empty" here or there, but rather as a force throughout, as a play of forces and waves of forces, at the same time one and many, increasing here, and at the same time decreasing there; a sea of forces flowing and rushing together, eternally changing, eternally flooding back, with tremendous years of recurrence, with an ebb of flow of its forms; out of the simplest forms striving towards the most complex, out of the stillest, most rigid, coldest forms towards the hottest, most turbulent, most self-contradictory, and then again returning home to the simple out of this abundance, out of the play of contradictions back to the joy of concord, still affirming itself in this uniformity of its courses and its years, blessing itself as that which must return eternally, as a becoming that knows no satiety, no disgust, no weariness: this, my Dionysian world of the eternally self creating, the eternally self-destroying, this mystery world of the twofold voluptuous delight, my "beyond good and evil," without goal, unless the joy of the circle is itself a goal; without will, unless a ring feels good will towards itself—do you want a name for this world? A solution for all its riddles? A light for you, too, you best-concealed, strongest, most intrepid, most midnightly men?—This world is the will to power—and nothing besides! Friedrich Nietzsche—*Will to Power*[2]

This text speaks almost graphically, destroying at the stroke of a pen the harmonic conception of nature constructed by Alexander von Humboldt. The destruction was carried out in

[2] Nietzsche, F., Hill, R. K., & Scarpitti, M. A. (2017). *The will to power: Selections from the notebooks of the 1880s*. Penguin Books.

the realm of philosophy through the questioning of the supposed cultural equilibrium of classical Greece understood by the same author as a violent struggle between antagonistic Apollonian and Dionysian tendencies in *The Birth of Tragedy*[3] (1872). This redescription would be followed by the destruction of historical time, by the eternal return, and by the new man who can only emerge from the ruins of all inherited order. These theses hardly offer much in the way of survival strategies, but there is one that is clearly formulated in *The Birth of Tragedy*: "only as an *aesthetic phenomenon* are existence and the world *justified* to eternity," a phrase that transports us to the milieu around Pont-Aven, particularly to Vincent van Gogh, who with *The Starry Night* (1889) had made of plein air painting a genre that fit so well with this Nietzschean conception that it could be viewed as a fantastic illustration of the Nietzschean description of the world. Once Turner had eliminated the compositional close-up, the frame came to be a window through which the artist moved. The artist paints himself by way of the landscape, transferring his interior world to the subject matter, thus conferring a highly symbolic expressive value to the subjective deformation of form and color.

Van Gogh's *The Starry Night* reflects this world of eternal circularity—"without goal, unless the joy of the circle is itself a goal"—that allows us to enter Bruno Taut's *Alpine Architecture*,[4] a book of watercolors and drawings with a number of written annotations that in some ways marks the (brief) triumph of German Expressionism. *Alpine Architecture*, which Taut wrote after having published his more formally traditional *The City Crown*[5] (1919), is a theatrical essay, an initiation to Expressionism that invites us to set off on an almost mystical journey toward cosmogonic and hallucinatory visions of a new architecture not just inspired by but literally fused with the landscape of the summits of the Alps.

It's curious that this book was published in 1919, the year in which our second protagonist here, Antonio Palacios, developed his proposal for the competition for the Círculo de Bellas Artes in Madrid, whose construction would last until the year 1926, continually beset by conflicts and problems. With Palacios, nothing was ever gentle and smooth: he was a combative figure with a heroic streak in his attitude as an architect. I will also speak about the Círculo de Bellas

3   Nietzsche, F. (1994, orig. 1872). *The Birth of Tragedy*. Penguin Classics.
4   Taut, B. (1919). *Alpine architektur: in 5 teilen und 30 zeichnungen des architekten*. Hogeni.
5   Taut, B. (1919). *Die Stadtkrone*. E. Diedrichs.

Artes as one of the most delirious attempts at creating a skyscraper that has ever been made, and certainly the most delirious one created in Spain in that era. And it was in the very same year, 1926, that construction commenced on the Telefónica Building on Madrid's then-new Gran Vía, the great metropolitan axis that inaugurated the twentieth century in Madrid and which just recently—in 2010—celebrated 100 years since construction work began on the street. The Telefónica Building would be the first Spanish skyscraper in a

The Starry Night, Vincent van Gogh. 1889

genuinely American style; based on the technical recommendations of the ITT corporation, it was constructed at the highest point on Gran Vía, and one of the most elevated points in the entire city. As such, it became a kind of observatory and one of the icons of the modernization of Madrid, crowning a glittering Gran Vía, on which the new typologies of hotels, commercial buildings, and offices were being erected, which drastically transformed the appearance of the city.

A text about the Círculo de Bellas Artes, an exhibition featuring the originals of *Alpine Architecture*, and an intervention in the Telefónica Building in which we propose a radical transformation inspired by Taut and Palacios, all works in which I was directly implicated, form the connective, somewhat delirious thread of this tripartite essay, which is primarily about the potentials of skyscrapers that largely lay dormant within modernity.

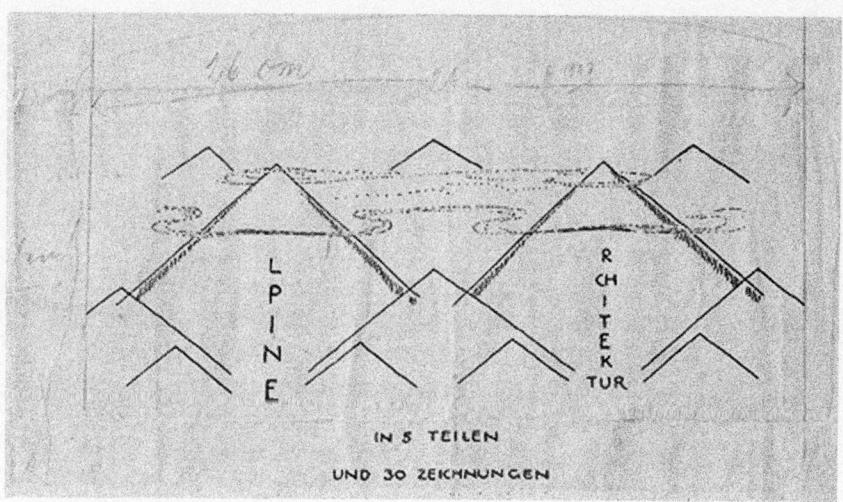

Bruno Taut, *Alpine Architecture*, in five parts and thirty illustrations

1. Alpine Aphorisms (1917–1919)

Bruno Taut's fantasies of *Alpine Architecture* should not be situated in the past but in the present, as anticipations of the future, and particularly as anticipations of a new form of understanding vertical constructions, capable of balancing out the problems of the ultra-dense metropolises that are flourishing as the globalized mode of living in the twenty-first century. While the canonical form of modern skyscrapers was essentially a structure for optimizing bureaucratic work conceptualized to stand out against the backdrop of the traditional cityscape, underscoring the power of large corporations (not to mention their obviously phallic symbolism), today, a century later, we find ourselves confronted by cities in which, more than anything else, verticality has come to be the most characteristic and widespread construction and typological system, both background and figure, the new topography of the global city. Height as a mechanism of isolation, and the symbiosis between nature and artificial creation are themes that Nietzsche—and not just Paul Scheerbart—identified in his widely cited aphorism "Architecture for the Search for Knowledge" in *The Gay Science*. The extent to which these elements are aesthetically rooted in Romanticism and the Picturesque should not be underestimated. They form the two central axes of *Alpine Architecture*, in that it proposes an architecture that is transmuted into human nature and ceases to be divine, even if they are largely inspired by Gothic structures, just as Romantic authors had interpreted them before they were subsequently taken up by the Expressionists. As Nietzsche writes:

> The time is past when the church possessed a monopoly on reflection, when the *vita contemplativa* always had to be first of all a *vita religiosa*; and everything built by the church gives expression to that idea. I do not see how we could remain content with such buildings even if they were stripped of their churchly purposes. The language spoken by these buildings is far too rhetorical and unfree, reminding us that they are houses of God and ostentatious monuments of some supramundane intercourse; we who are godless could not think *our thoughts* in such surroundings. We wish to see *ourselves* translated into stone and plants, we want to take walks *in ourselves* when we stroll around these buildings and gardens.[6]

The second section of *Alpine Architecture* is the one that interests me most here, because it is a genuine manual about the modes and manners in which architecture and nature could be reconnected from an Expressionist and nihilist perspective. While the other sections of the book can be interpreted as an ambitious treatise organized in a theatrical manner, the second one pauses on the more technical aspects of the formal repertoire and its thematic

6   Nietzsche, F. (1974). *The gay science*. Vintage Books.

and compositional organization, on laying out the instruments and laws of composition of a new architecture for the search for knowledge. For this reason, its structure is not linear like that of the rest of the work, whose trajectory commences in a mountain lake around which, ascending

Bruno Taut, *Alpine Architecture*, illustration 21

as if part of an initiation, we arrive successively at a fusion of the alpine, the terrestrial, and the cosmic, while we progress in our reading and contemplation of its various parts.
In this second part, the progression pauses and the seven illustrations are organized like a catalog or a travel guide for the initiated that specifies the practical application of a limited repertoire in which the alpine topographies—the

bottom of the valley, the summits, the courses and forms of the water, and the geomorphological and atmospheric materiality—distil forms and paradigmatic prototypes that

Bruno Taut, *Alpine Architecture*, illustration 7, "The Crystal Mountain"

can be replicated and in which we can recognize the most relevant characteristics as the imprint of alpine verticality and the tension between collective creation and spiritual isolation which this imprint brings with it.

The ornamental motif that introduces part two is a concise foretaste of what is to follow, with its artificially symmetrical nature and the water vapor of the clouds forming ascending halos that encircle the triangular peaks, a composition that is then elaborated in illustrations 5, 7, and 8, each with different focuses but all with two common motifs: the gem-like summits with triangular and polyhedral facets whose crystalline associations are not difficult to identify, and rectangular mountaintops and hills that lead to emergent arcades forming the virtual latticework of a dome, or rather, when open toward the firmament, forming the filigree of a chalice. Additionally, the ascending halo lends the three illustrations a nebulous air that erases all other attention. As we know, these two motifs respond in a formal key to the writings of the mystic Meister Erkhardt on the transcendent nature of the dualism of the feminine and the masculine. However, the repertoire was not limited to this somewhat obvious or literal system, which certainly sums up Taut's emotional state after fleeing Katowice with his daughter's teacher; rather, toward the bottom of illustration 7 and in the main component of illustration 9, other architectural forms are depicted, exhibiting a different geometry, rectangular and terraced, coinciding with their location at the bottom of the valley, the place where the snow and the vapor of the clouds transform into water in its liquid state and into movement, giving way to a third geometrical typology that evokes Babylonian, Incan, or Aztec architectures, as well as having a certain resemblance to the palaces of Nepal. On the other hand, in illustrations 6 and 10, the bottom of the valley triggers in Taut's imagination another, fourth pattern in the form of floral formations that have symbolism of a clearly sexual, feminine nature, with all of this allowing us to think that while in the heights the triangular and arced forms mimic the masculine/feminine dualism of the alpine orography, in the valleys, the terraced slopes with waterfalls or colorful floral forms serve as a dual correlate adapted to an expansive—horizontal—mode of construction, instead of an intensive, vertical one.

The transmutation of architecture into transcendent human nature would thus have four formal principles—triangulations, archways, terracing, and floral formations—and a single thread connecting it all: water in its liquid, solid, and gaseous states, tying together these patterns in a vital and physical continuum. But the clarity of the scheme and of its references partially disappears when we compare illustrations 7 and 8

("The Crystal Mountain" and "Grotesque Region"), since here the same motifs develop in two highly divergent aesthetic keys, for if the first is figurative and disconcertingly

Bruno Taut, *Alpine Architecture*, illustration 22
Bruno Taut, "Solar System," illustration 28, original number lost. From the printed edition of *Alpine Architecture*

symmetrical, the second materializes in the key of Cubist abstraction, making even of the clouds a kind of concertina ramp, with the whole ensemble thus generating a dramatic tension that is different to the first, whose formal stasis achieves a kind of drama by way of its bizarre perfectionism, which calls to mind something oneiric or surreal (a little bit *Twin Peaks*, to give you an idea). Throughout the entire book we encounter reiterations of this other dualism between the figurative and abstraction, between classical formal order and more daring sculptural experiments—see, for example, illustrations 21, 22, and 29, which I consider to be more interesting precisely because they diverge more strongly from the imitation of nature and propose forms that have probably never before been imagined. On the other hand, it seems evident that this other dualism—between the historicist ambitions of the author, which are embodied clearly in *The City Crown* written a few years earlier, and his attention to the vanguards, abstract and Expressionist—is consubstantial with his entire aesthetic project, with its roots buried in the Picturesque and Romantic conceptions that sought to create a unified canon for natural phenomena and human creations, while at the same time being profoundly imbued with the pessimism and subjectivism that Expressionism represented as a reaction to the positivist faith in progress and its brutal "adverse effects" in the First World War, which demanded another way of situating the subject in the world, in nature.

Without a doubt, whether consciously or not, this system of formal patterns is present in much of today's interesting architecture—and it is openly present in the work that we have been developing in our studio—as well as being patently present in the fascination in a vitreous materiality, in the color or the vertical connections along inclined planes forming ascending ramps. All of these elements have an extreme vitality in contemporary architecture, a vitality which, almost a century later, deserves the attention of critics and the broader public alike. I don't believe it is necessary to insist on this, as it is plainly evident. Rather we should focus on the crucial difference that Bruno Taut's ideational process supposes, an ambitious cosmogonic construction that connects the culture of architecture, history, new sculptural tendencies, new visions of nature, and lines of coetaneous philosophical thought by way of a visionary deployment of the imagination and the use of that somatic medium that is the sketch or hand made drawing. As did Le Corbusier shortly thereafter, Taut needed the holistic construction of a new, imaginary world from which he could project himself into reality. And at the same time, he was conscious of the limits of logocentrism, of reason and reasoning, opposing the rationalist faith of functionalism with a method close to that of Nietzsche's aphorisms, based on the initiatory journey and rhetorical

Bruno Taut, *Alpine Architecture*, illustration 9, "Valley with Ornate Architecture"

persuasion in opposition to the formal logical structure of syllogism. Possessing the quality of graphic aphorisms, the persuasive force of Taut's illustrations is based not just on their laudable skill but also on their open nature;

indeed they almost seem disjointed, with lines that sketch out figures but do not complete them, lines that do not converge in points but slip over one another or never quite come into contact, eluding all yearning for precision, letting not just his own imagination roam but the imaginations of those who find themselves trapped in this evanescent atmosphere, completed only in their minds. This double approach to the project—the creation of a fantastical cosmogony and the recourse to a technique that we could

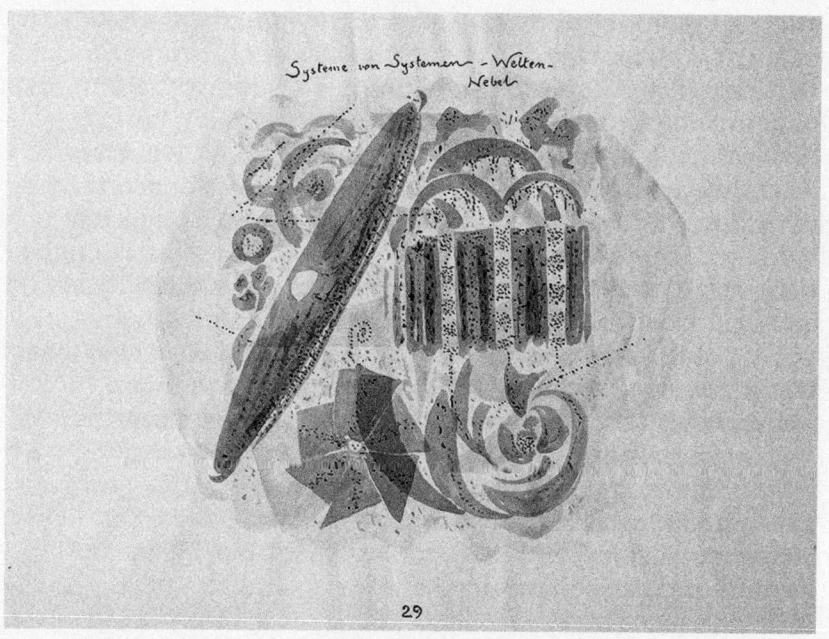

Bruno Taut, *Alpine Architecture*, illustration 29, "Systems of Systems—Worlds—Clouds"

call sculptural aphorisms—constitutes an exercise whose validity and efficacy would be worth thinking about today, since although it is true that many things have changed, what hasn't changed is the uncertainty about the future and the definition of the role of the individual and creativity in an overcrowded context that is saturated with technology. If anything, these factors have intensified, unveiling even more strikingly the limits of reason when it comes to providing satisfactory answers to contemporary urban concerns.

Anybody who carefully approaches this seemingly simple and captivatingly spontaneous book enters little by little into an incredibly well-structured universe, the product of a creative mind of enormous talent, whose drive toward the construction of a new notion of beauty permits him to enter into territories that are virtually inaccessible by any means other than those that structure the book—the rite of passage, the visionary exercise of the imagination, and the surrender to the somatic medium of the hand—creating a series of persuasive aphorisms that construct a cosmogonic vision of architecture.

(As a final aside: I cannot conceal the fact that all of these themes have had an influence on our work. In the first project we had the opportunity to realize at the foot of the Alps, in Turin, with just this kind of complex vertical program, we felt the need to reminisce on Taut's crystalline structures, twisting and looking toward the mountains from the rationality of the urban fabric of Turin. Likewise, when we have had to construct subterranean structures or grottoes, as at the Intermodal Station in Logroño (La Rioja, Spain), we accommodated triangular facets inspired by the drawings of Bruno Taut, decomposing planes and generating an ambivalence between the grotto—made of lightweight sheets of aluminum profile—and the garden above it, whose flower beds have the same triangular pattern as the hollow space below, created with natural materials rather than artificial ones. Recto and verso, heads and tails, between the natural and the artificial, the mountain and the cave, these two projects unabashedly illustrate Taut's influence, displaying it with the satisfaction of being associated with something one loves.)

2. A Delirious Circle[7] (1919–1926)

The Círculo de Bellas Artes in Madrid, a work by Antonio Palacios, is linked temporally with Bruno Taut's treatise, with the competition for its design being announced in 1919 and the work being completed in 1926. Antonio Palacios (1874–1945) was an architectural paradox, being highly criticized during his lifetime and only recently recognized as having created the most unique works in the city of Madrid, works which give the city a metropolitan and cosmopolitan character.

[7] The text on which this translation is based is an edited version of the text "Un Círculo Delirante," published in volume 40 of "Arquitectura española del siglo XX" in the illustrated encyclopedia *Summa Artis* (1996), the catalog to the exhibition *Antonio Palacios, constructor de Madrid* (2001), and the book *Essays on Thermodynamics, Architecture and Beauty* (2015).

But the fortunes of some buildings are largely determined by the ability of the critics of the age—and of ensuing eras— to absorb the ideas contained within them. And by the

Spina Tower in Turin, Ábalos+Sentkiewicz. Italy, 2008
Intermodal Station in Logroño, Ábalos+Sentkiewicz. Spain, 2006–2020

coherence and the rigor their creators, by their ability to elaborate a trajectory that mirrors, and is tailored to, the problems of the epoch, to the ideas being proposed by the cultural debate at any given moment. With the Círculo de

Bellas Artes and the figure of Antonio Palacios, we find the very opposite. Both the architect and his work can be viewed as examples of an untimely attitude. It would be difficult for us to speak of a coherent creator, and there was also no critical model in his epoch to support his work. The Círculo was completed just as modernity was really beginning to yield its most remarkable accomplishments internationally; neither the vindication of functional ideas nor the currents based on the reconsideration of an autochthonous tradition would be able to offer conceptual support to the Círculo, which in its time was met with moderate praise, but always with reservations. Among both the Modernists and the traditionalists, it represented a superficial monumentalism, a nostalgic and individualist attitude realized by an architect who was highly gifted but narcissistic and self-sufficient. Although nobody would question Palacios's mastery of his vocation, both the building and its designer would be left to the winds of fate. And it is surprising to confirm that this has essentially remained the case to this day, as is evinced by the definition of Palacios as a "compulsive formalizer" in the volume of *Summa Artis* recently dedicated to Spanish twentieth-century architecture.

But sometimes it happens that the development of critical ideas eventually catches up to buildings of the past that had not yet found their interpretive model, and these designs then appear as if bathed in a new light. It's the moment of "I've always said that …," of the rearticulation of popular forms of knowledge in academic formulas, of the rearrangement of academic study and urban guides. I think that, fortunately, something similar might be happening to the Círculo de Bellas Artes in Madrid, and that a part of the responsibility for this growing positive assessment resides in the abandonment of a simplistic critical model that was resistant to a reconsideration of figures whose ideologies were at odds with those of the historian. Such is the case with Palacios, about whom we can say that his untimely character was untimely in all directions—since he went through a whole range of ideological shifts throughout his biography—and that the casting aside of this model has brought an important break for his work. Today, we can see it without these kinds of filters, freed of the oppressive presence of his "father," allowing it to appear to us just as it is, as an artifact, as a dazzling piece of architecture in dialogue with the physical medium that supports it. But another, even more significant portion of the responsibility for the transformation of the contemporary perspective on his work comes from the recent emergence of a vision of the modern metropolis in which its disorder and congestion are understood as necessary and desirable elements, for which ethical and moral criteria based on reformist

View of the Círculo de Bellas Artes from Cibeles, Madrid, ca. 1920

visions demanding a harmonious order no longer apply—as was certainly the case with Modernist orthodoxy, from the first texts by Le Corbusier to the Athens Charter—and are replaced by criteria of scientific observation and interpretation, in search of the hidden orders in the chaos that is played out in modern metropolises. Books such as *Los Angeles: The Architecture of Four Ecologies* by Reyner

Banham, or the later *Delirious New York* by Rem Koolhaas—standard reading for architectural students around the world—have paved the way for an appreciation of that which the latter author terms the "culture of congestion." This paradigm is exemplified in the Downtown Athletic Club of New York, a skyscraper constructed in 1931, whose extraordinarily complex program—which included a hotel, gymnasium, swimming pools, squash courts, and even a miniature golf course, each with their own floor—exhibits the forms in which the artificial experience of the ambience of the metropolis crystallizes: its delirious dimension. It is no coincidence that I am mentioning this New York

Antonio Palacios on the rooftop of his studio on Calle Cedaceros in Madrid, ca. 1930

skyscraper in my discussion of the Círculo de Bellas Artes. When, a few years ago, we proposed the Círculo as an object of study to the students at the School of Architecture in Madrid, the first comparative analysis they unanimously proposed for it was with the Downtown Athletic Club, closely followed by the Auditorium in Chicago, a work by Louis H. Sullivan, another great structure of similar programmatic complexity that vertically organizes the uses that would traditionally unfurl across the two-dimensional expanse of the city.

This unanimity is telling for many reasons. Firstly, because it points directly to the North American metropolis as a precursor to this great constructed dream that is the Círculo, and to the skyscraper in its most primitive North American

forms as the typological model. Secondly, because it suggests
what might be the most adequate interpretive model
with which to proceed to use and restore this building, and

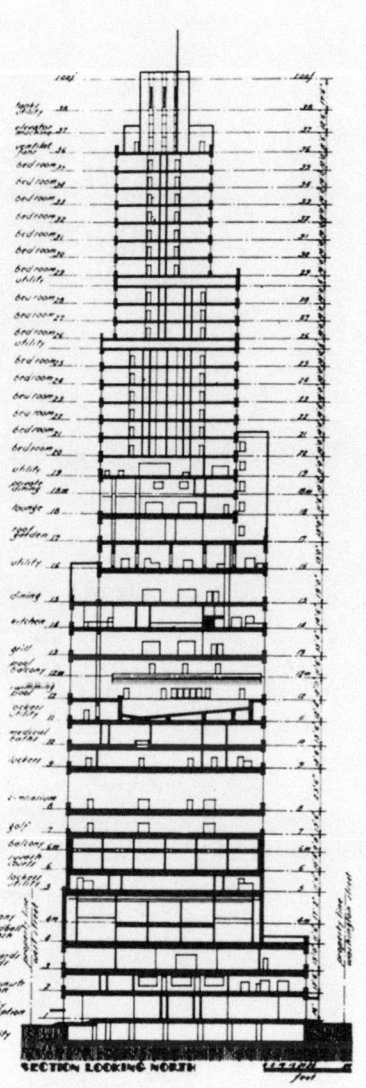

Downtown Athletic Club, Starrett & van Vleck. New York, 1930

to endow it with urban content. And finally, because it
demonstrates the relevance of the Círculo, a relevance that
refers not only to the present but also to the moment
in which it was designed, given that Palacios's project was

conceived in 1919 and the work was completed in 1926, while the Downtown Athletic Club was created in 1931.

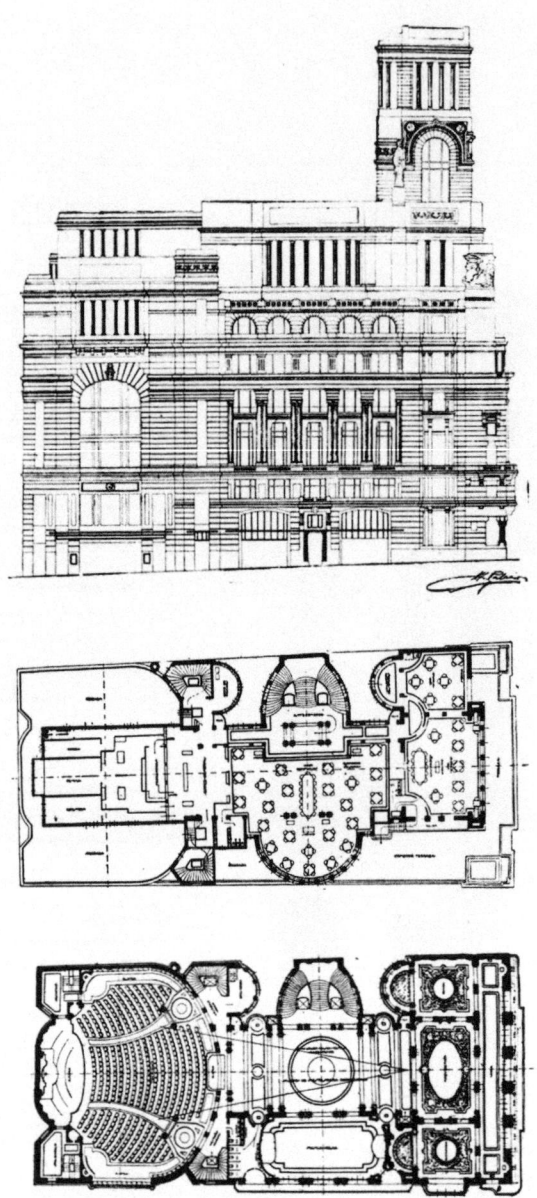

Street elevation, first upper floor, and main floor in the proposal by Antonio Palacios, 1919

As we know, the project was the result of an eventful competition that was presented with two opposing designs, embodied in the examples of Secundino Zuazo and Antonio Palacios. Comparing the drawings from the proposals

submitted, we clearly see two radically different conceptions
of the singular program that was proposed. For Zuazo,
the Círculo was an administrative building; it was a guild

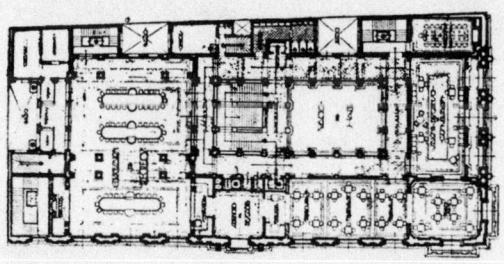

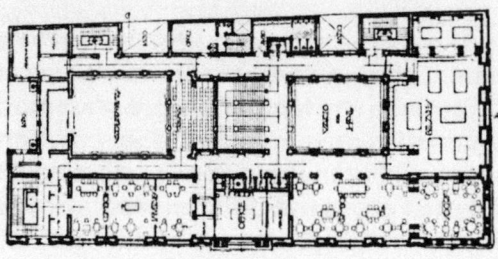

Street elevation, main floor, and mezzanine in the proposal by Secundino Zuazo and Fernández Quintanilla, 1919

organization and therefore accommodated the typical
mechanisms of these buildings—and of social clubs—by way
of corridors around patios and atria manipulated with
great mastery to render a harmonic succession of spaces

that have an essentially two-dimensional and organizational origin. Palacios's design abandons patios, corridors, and other repetitive forms; the building is interpreted as a vertical explosion of different kinds of spaces that jostle for position, propped up against one another, as occurs with the cupola that spans the entire library and ends up transformed into a fountain next to the column hall. It is an almost Expressionist, Babylonian exercise, of an enormous violence and vertical thrust, in which the designer struggles to domesticate an

Photographs of the interior of the Círculo de Bellas Artes, 1926. Main lobby, member access, indoor pool in the basement, ballroom, members' dining room, and the "little fountain" or smoking room in the main recreation room

organizational type that finds its references in Chicago and in a positive attitude in the face of the programmatic complexity, which is no longer approached as an attempt to reach agreements but instead in a way that seeks to exasperate and express the differences three-dimensionally. This is surely the conceptual core of the Círculo, an intimation of a skyscraper, the first in Madrid, at a location where the most metropolitan urban systems of the early twentieth century converge: Calle Alcalá and the recently unveiled Gran Vía. Its position and imposing presence in the city adds expressive power to its vertical thrust: while toward Calle Alcalá it maintains a certain urban modesty, with the ordered and richly ornamental composition of its lower sections, it explodes toward the summit into an almost Piranesian ensemble of forms and geometries of an abstract vernacular—art deco—that culminates in the famous tower of studios that even today continues to protrude above the city skyline, and that caused so many legal problems for Palacios, who managed to ultimately overcome the opposition to it and complete it, demonstrating not just the importance that he conferred to this compositional element

but also his identification with the act of rebellion and individualism that it signified in the city. It is a self-sufficient and vertical structure that, though it does maintain a certain decorum in its encounter with the street, measures itself primarily against the topography of Madrid, against the Retiro Park and the Plaza de Cibeles, against the Paseo del Prado and Gran Vía, against the most singular elements of the city it faces, which, in an anthropomorphic stance, it "squares off" against. In the same way the Pallas Athena that Juan Luis Vasallo molded in bronze and that Palacios positioned to crown his construction "squares off" against the tower and the building in its entirety, with which it harbors not just compositional similarities in its vertical thrust and its position—dominating the city—but also symbolic similarities: Pallas Athena, the goddess of the arts and of war, "golden and triumphant" in the words of Palacios, represents the struggle of the artist that he imagined himself to be and which the building of the Círculo de Bellas Artes symbolizes, a building that dominates the city, making art triumph within it.

The artist Palacios sought to accommodate with his building was not a bureaucrat with professional problems, but a cosmopolitan figure, a flâneur, Charles Baudelaire's artist of modern life who strolls along the avenues and sits on the terraces to chat and to observe the nervous pulse of the great city. His rooms are organized as a sequence of spaces linked together into floors and sections without being resolved into a continuity, in which the "conversation" is the most prominent program, unequivocally betraying an aristocratic conception of artistic practice with which Palacios felt comfortable, as did the artists who, through their insistence, managed to eventually push through his proposal over that of Zuazo. One only need glance at the program imagined and constructed by Palacios to understand the reach of this conception. Lower floor: lobbies, exhibition space, conversation room, and sunroom. Mezzanine: intimate life of the club, small recreation rooms, and sunroom. Main floor: large festivities, meeting and conversation rooms, theater, and cinema. First loft: library. Second loft: recreation room and management. First floor terraces: dining rooms and kitchens. Second floor terraces: fine arts. First basement: physical education, bar, bathrooms, gymnasium, fencing, and "skating rink." It is no coincidence, therefore, that people automatically associate this building with the Downtown Athletic Club, which is today a celebrated work of architecture, since both projects are animated by the same spirit. Moreover, certain uses of language and space link it with Sullivan's Auditorium in Chicago, whose tower follows a similar compositional scheme, where, incidentally, Sullivan had his own studio.

By way of these links, which though they might be somewhat anecdotal are nevertheless important in the context of the evolution of architectural criticism, this work has opened itself up to a new interpretation, in which it resurges as one of the exceedingly rare examples in Madrid of a cosmopolitan and excessive architecture, divorced from the reformist moralism of functionalist currents, but attentive to all those aspects of modernity that today form our most accurate understanding of what the twentieth-century city has come to be.

Heterodox and untimely, Palacios left us an admirable building—perhaps his most rounded and perfect work—whose critical fortune has been hamstrung but whose present and future now appear bright, recognized as the best and most lucid exercise of modernity that Madrid attempted in the early twentieth century.

3. The Vertical Park[8] (1926–1929)

The opportunity to curate the exhibition *Arquitectura Alpina* and edit the accompanying catalog at Antonio Palacios's Círculo de Bellas Artes in the spring of 2011, exhibiting Bruno Taut's original illustrations, and to curate the exhibition *Laboratorio Gran Vía* at the Telefónica Building, which in 2010 was celebrating 100 years since the construction of Madrid's Gran Vía began, provided the chance to posit a relation between both buildings, and to use the latter as an experimental project in which the influence of Taut and Palacios is made manifest, making way for an experiment investigating how to transform the modern office skyscraper into an observatory and museum, an experiment which brings to a close these three episodes, which are linked together by curious temporal and spatial concatenations. The exhibition *Laboratorio Gran Vía*, held on the fifth floor of the Telefónica Building, arranged the dislocated course of Gran Vía over the length of the floor in twelve sections, the same number of Madrid studios invited to make proposals for the future of Gran Vía. In our case, it was inevitable that we would choose to redesign the very building hosting the exhibition, which was originally designed by Ignacio de Cárdenas under the supervision of Louis S. Weeks, who conceived numerous buildings for ITT and was an expert in this typology. It was clear to us from the first moment that in terms of its typology, the building is the antithesis of the Círculo de Bellas Artes. The two (proto-)skyscrapers, separated by a mere 500 meters, and facing each other from their terraced roofs, exhibit the most evident difference

---

8   This text gathers together fragments of documents included in the catalog to the exhibition *Laboratorio Gran Vía* (2010), curated by the author as part of the project presented by Ábalos+Sentkiewicz in the aforementioned exhibition, and from the text "El Parque Vertical" published in *Babelia*, a weekly cultural supplement in *El País*, on January 17, 2009.

between the bureaucratic vocation of the modern skyscraper, orthodoxly Taylorist right down to its rationalized methods of construction, devoted to the circulation of people and the organization of flows of information—a model that reached its apogee at the hands of the taciturn and admirable American Mies van der Rohe—and the delirious or Babylonian model of skyscrapers which are above all a celebration of the communion between the city, nature, and culture, a communion that precisely these palaces of modernity can

Telefónica Building during its construction, viewed from the Círculo de Bellas Artes, 1927

bring about, enriching the human condition, human knowledge, and creativity by connecting us with the world, just as observatories do or the Círculo de Bellas Artes does, transforming our primary visual experience by way of specific technologies of knowledge.

In the original documentation of the Telefónica Building, whose construction was initiated just as the Círculo de Bellas Artes was approaching completion, and in particular the photographs of its construction following the typological and technological models that already existed for office buildings—and more specifically offices and telephone exchanges—the image that truly stands out for its striking beauty is the one of the riveted reticular structure that emerges above the city at its most elevated point, showing that at any moment, before being enveloped in bureaucratic garb and Plateresque ornament, this innovative structure had (and still retains today) a surprisingly beautiful nature, erected on top of this base that the city of Madrid represents for it.

We interpret it as a rock—here, Bruno Taut returns, emerging from that geological support and that reticular, stepped structure—provoking us to transform the Telefónica Building into a mineral park, a mountain that is accessible from within and without, from above and below: a new, mechanized garden of the twenty-first century. In this way, we proposed a thoroughgoing restructuring of the building at the programmatic and typological level, and as a conduit of public activity in the city. The objective is not just to transform the original structure of the first high-rise office block in Spain into a huge center of investigation into the relations between science, art, and technology, but also to drastically modify the typically introverted character of the offices using the resources that already exist in the building in order to convert it into an extroverted structure, one that is public and fully accessible, inserted into the fabric of the city, as well as to convert it into a new museum type and a vertical garden, a rock to be climbed, and from the summit of which one can contemplate and get to know the city. An observatory looking outward and inward, whose section and program are organized according to thematic scales in homage to the book and film *Powers of Ten* by Ray and Charles Eames: cosmos, earth, city, man, DNA, and atom. The project that we carried out illustrates the "vertical park," a micro-essay about the roots of ideas that have emerged over the past decades, marking the evolution of high-rise construction in the contemporary city:

> What we understand as a park is born at the moment in which somebody traces a sinusoidal path, traversing an untouched fragment of nature, and discovers how attractive it is to arrange the space such that the direction of the eye and the feet never coincide, that the paths circle around the object of vision and construct a scenography of the gaze and a ballet of the mobility of the body. This is the elemental, two-

dimensional principle of an "experiential" interest that was inaugurated back in the late eighteenth century as a theme of aesthetic order, as a new form of empirically founded beauty, an idea that modernity re-elaborated one hundred years later, introducing these paths into buildings—Le Corbusier accurately called them *promenades architecturales*, and with these, he traversed his projects, which transformed into cinematic still lifes, finding a duplicate of the Picturesque garden in the interior of his works of architecture (the window-landscapes both united and separated the outside—framing the gardens—and the inside—the Cubist still lifes—two sides of the one conception that expanded the ballet and the sinusoidal scenography to a third dimension). Today, landscape architecture has come to accommodate the most complex forms, incorporating new sculptural references, new techniques and materials, new scientific paradigms, and new dimensions, with the incorporation of time as an instrument of design and construction. The history of this sinusoidal line in architecture and landscape architecture is yet to be written, but we have also not yet imagined what such an expansion of the spatio-temporal possibilities of these two disciplines could offer in the near future. We will discover something if we look at the place where the ideas emerge, the incubators that are the schools of architecture and landscape architecture. There, the sinusoidal line inaugurated by the first Picturesque authors is currently receiving vertiginous levels of attention and undergoing a profound evolution. Regardless of where we go, regardless of the country or professor, the school or the dominant tendency, the architects of the future are attempting and unconsciously repeating a gesture that continues to be thwarted and is almost never successful, but with the obstinacy that is only produced by being obsessed with an idea that "has" to be done, and which continues to assert itself as necessary. And what is modeled with this reiteration is something that is difficult to catalog in the compartments of "architecture" or "landscape

Three Delirious Skyscrapers

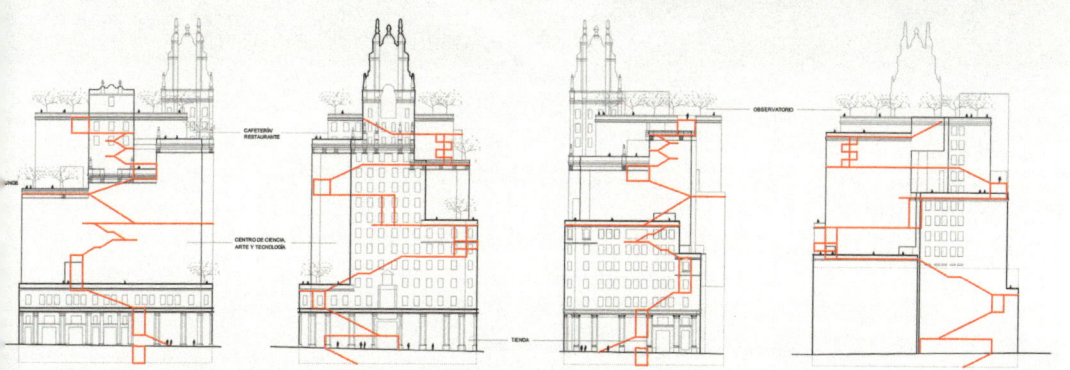

Images from the project "Telefónica Observatory," Ábalos+Sentkiewicz. Madrid, 2010

Image from the project "Telefónica Observatory," Ábalos+Sentkiewicz. Madrid, 2010

architecture," because it stubbornly seeks to meld both, twisting itself into helixes or nests, baskets or tornados. It seeks to construct a fresh hybrid entity, one that *is* vertical, but it is only out of habit that we could still call it a vertical structure or a "skyscraper." This vertical "entity" is a material that is at once natural and artificial, and seeks, by mechanizing its sinusoidal connection, to construct an analog experience to that which our modern maestros called the park, public space. In twisting itself, it generates a different kind of nature whose manipulation allows for the construction of hybrid programs of production and leisure, creating at the same time ecosystems, natural or theme parks, mazes, agricultural land and livestock farms, energetic parks that are self-sufficient, and open "entities" that use the wind, water, light, or the earth as active materials of construction, capable of generating public and economic resources. This vertical amalgam is without a doubt a new entity that is adapted to a new form of perception and a new notion of leisure; an entity that will allow for the establishment of new dialogues between humans and non-humans, generating a new "parliament of things," to borrow Bruno Latour's turn of phrase (whose influence is by no means insignificant). In this construct, the necessary integration of architecture, landscape, and environment emerges in an idealized form. It is, if you like, the culmination of these disciplines. And this is where its interest resides, in being at once origin and final crystallization of an understanding of design and the surrounding environment capable of melding three disciplines—architecture, landscape, and environment—into a new idea of public space and, if you like, into a monument in which both natural and artificial elements, as systems of capturing energy, materialize a hybrid prototype. It is not difficult to predict that we will see this idea constructed in just a few years, as the result of a design concept that is more than 200 years old. The ultimate park will be vertical, it will be constructed in all the major metropolises and will give new

188 Three Delirious Skyscrapers

Image from the project "Telefónica Observatory," Ábalos+Sentkiewicz. Madrid, 2010

life to the encounter between architecture and landscape architecture as disciplines of public space and the environment.[9]

I'd like to end this tour through 100 years of architectural history with a chart that seeks to illustrate the evolution in modes of thinking about and designing high-rise constructions, a table that is deliberately simplistic and provocative, but effectively demonstrates the evolution of skyscrapers as communal palaces of contemporary societies.

Twentieth century		Twenty-first century
Floor	Key Document	Section
Singular function	Program	Mixed usages
Tectonic	Design Technique	Thermodynamic
Exterior	Compositional Focus	Interior
Figure	Tool	Matter
Slender	Form	Massive
Top/crown	Max. Urban Intensity	Base/infrastructure
Figure/background contrast	Relation with the context	Figure and background
Control	Position of the subject	Knowledge
Future vs. present	Historical Projection	Past vs. present
Unique	Materiality	Hybrid

Bibliography:
Ábalos, I. (2010). *Laboratorio Gran Vía*. Fundación Telefónica.
Ábalos, I. & Taut, B. (1997). *Bruno Taut: Escritos Expresionistas*. El Croquis Editorial.
Banham, R. (1971). *Los Angeles: The architecture of four ecologies*. Harper and Row.
Koolhaas, R. (1994). *Delirious New York: A retroactive manifesto for Manhattan* (New ed.). New York: Monacelli Press.
Nietzsche, F. (1994, orig. 1872). *The birth of tragedy*. Penguin Classics.
Nietzsche, F. (1974). *The gay science*. Vintage Books.
Nietzsche, F., Hill, R. K., & Scarpitti, M. A. (2017). *The will to power: Selections from the notebooks of the 1880s*. Penguin Books.
Taut, B. (1919). *Die Stadtkrone*. E. Diedrichs.
Taut, B. (1919). *Alpine architektur: in 5 teilen und 30 zeichnungen des architekten*. Hogeni.
Taut, B. (1920). *Der Weltbaumeister: Architektur-Schauspiel für symphonische Musik, dem Geiste Paul Scheerbarts gewidmet*. Folkwang-Verlag.
Taut, B. (1920). *Die Auflösung der Städte; oder, Die Erde eine gute Wohnung; oder auch*. Erschienen im Folkwang.
VV.AA. (1919). "El Concurso de Anteproyectos para el Edificio del Círculo de Bellas Artes de Madrid." *Revista Architectura*, n. 16 (August).

9   Ábalos, I. (2009). "Verticalismo." *Babelia* (*El País*), January.

Dualisms

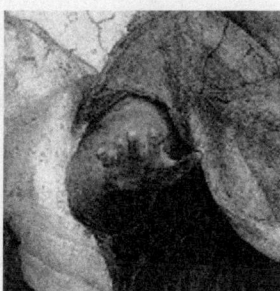

Detail of Plato and Aristotle in Raphael's *The School of Athens*, 1509–1511

1. Organization or Design?[1]

The two symposia "Design Techniques" and "Organization or Design?" responded in opposing ways to the same question: how do we construct the architectural project? This is a question that we pose in a pragmatic way, not so much from a theoretical point of view, but rather by observing work practices that are considered to be of interest from the two positions, both for students and for professors of one form of praxis or another. Academia has been—and continues to be—the best arena for these discussions, since it has to, on the one hand, generate and disseminate knowledge of tried and tested design techniques, and on the other hand, function as a laboratory for exploring other, alternative practices that claim to be more advanced, and which have begun to gain traction among teachers and students. This struggle is always pertinent within the academy, whose aim is both to disseminate the knowledge produced by the profession and to advance this knowledge base by exploring and discussing novel ideas in their most embryonic and speculative state.

The tension implied by the terms "design" and "organization" with respect to the work of an architect brought me to reflect upon the conversation between Plato and Aristotle captured so accurately by the palette and composition of the great Raphael in his fresco *The School of Athens*. In this fresco, Plato is depicted pointing with his index finger toward the sky, signaling toward the heavenly vaults reigned over by the supreme order of the cosmos, governed by rigid laws whose logic is often inaccessible to humans. In his left hand, he is holding *Timaeus*, his most abstract and ambitious work. Aristotle's hand is held out horizontally, with his palm facing toward the ground, toward the realm of human beings, of life, of human passions and emotions. This is also the sphere of agreements: an everyday world governed by ethics, as the fresco clearly makes evident by showing us Aristotle holding his own *Nicomachean Ethics* in his other hand. Trust in the scientific objectivity of the laws of the universe is set against human subjectivity and human impulses. There is little need to argue whether this duality still remains in the architectural dispute between its necessity to systematize and objectivize form and those approaches that underline the cultural character of

---

[1] Closing remarks at the third Symposium on Architecture: "Organization or Design?" held at Harvard GSD on October 15, 2015, as part of the "All that is solid…" symposia series.

the city and its built artifacts, expressions of a subjective creativity whose construction requires cultural rather than technical expertise.

If in "Design Techniques," greater emphasis was placed on grouping together the significant and very personal approaches of certain designers who have an unquestionable influence on the current international stage, this symposium on "Organization or Design?" reflects both on whether there is actually a method of design which is not based on the subjective idea of creativity and on whether a rigorous organization of information is able to convert certain parameters into organs (organizations) or buildings, and how this can be undertaken. Creating a structural division of the two symposia and the two resulting publications enables both approaches to outline their interests, methods, and achievements, eschewing confrontation and thus undermining not only counterproductive journalistic disputes but also any interest in reconciling the two approaches, since their very coexistence is understood to be both completely necessary and enriching, an entirely natural phenomenon. Indeed, we so often witness their productive coexistence within one and the same architect, for whom this coexistence recoils against the will and/or capacity of the architects with the most polarized standpoint to see and understand themselves.

Yet Raphael's painting surely shows us not two worlds but three, in that it brings together three ways of being in the world which could exemplify the way a project is developed. First, the way that trusts those abstract laws that rule over the great machine of the cosmos and the netherworld whose laws facilitate—insofar as they are actually comprehensible—the construction of ingenious structures which enable us to progress in terms of knowledge and efficacy by emulating the governance of the gods; second, the way that considers that our way of being in the world is among humans, establishing agreements and permitting the human spirit to express its subjectivity, since that subjectivity primarily lies in recognizing our own subjectivity and the sheer creative force of this; and third, an almost concealed way, that of Raphael himself, who constructs, for both ways of understanding, an environment composed of beautiful architectural frameworks made both of stone stands and floors and of ethereal vaults imitating the heavenly geometry, thus composing a fraternal framework centered around conversation—which for Raphael is the real subject matter, a topic of far greater importance than the actual arguments of the one or the other. Put simply, both the laws of science and human pacts, or their subjective ethics and aesthetics and dialectics, come together in this Raphael fresco whose title, *The School of Athens*, is quite deliberately chosen: the academy is above this or that author; it is this one, that one, and the one listening closely; those in the vicinity taking notes who will later go on to construct their

Raphael's *The School of Athens*, 1509–1511

own world. The academy is that essential place that allows architecture to primarily be a conversation, a city.

2. On Design Techniques[2]

The D in GSD has great significance in the culture of this institution insofar as it indicates that in order to get to the core of a discipline such as architecture, it is productive to not just think within the traditional boundaries of the discipline

[2] Introduction to the Symposium on Architecture: "Design Techniques I," held on October 30, 2014 at Harvard GSD, as part of the "All that is solid…" symposia series.

but also look outside, expanding the conventional limits of the discipline, coming into contact with other design disciplines which can help to break traditional conventions. Design is a term that undoubtedly encompasses many disciplines, forging a path toward a shared "outside." Both outward and inward motions are nevertheless necessary and complementary, the systoles and the diastoles of a system that grants us a certain vitality and enables us to plan for the future. Planning for the future involves to a certain extent pointing forward and saying "we're going that way."
It involves making the right decision, not only in terms of the profession agreeing but also in terms of taking social reality and cultural reality into consideration, including all their issues and aspirations, and adding a new idea of beauty to cultural material. None of this is achieved either by looking outward and pointing or by taking refuge in an unyielding disciplinary autonomy.

Yet perhaps we should start today with something a little more modest and necessary, and ask ourselves what we are doing, which design techniques really interest us, which ones do we believe in, which ones make us say: "I don't like those other ones any more, I don't believe in them, their time has come and gone, don't ask me why, I'm only doing what I believe I should be doing and hardly know how or why I'm doing it." How or why I am doing this, what and who inspires me are highly relevant and paradoxically opaque topics which are avoided in a profession whose culture is often too amused by the mighty words of philosophy and science.

I'd like to mention two points before moving on. Firstly, the importance of "how" and "why" is explained by attempting to identify that core moment that keeps architects (and students) absorbed and focused, enthralled by their profession, devoting countless hours to this "Aristotelian mover," design, which enables them to capture in one pleasurable moment a vast amount of initially chaotic data of all types and convert it into a vision that will take years or decades to materialize, coming up against countless problems along the way. For many this is an important moment; for the vast majority it is the single most important one, the moment that assigns meaning to architecture, the one that best expresses its dual condition as science and art, knowledge and subjectivity, the basic ingredients for building a meaningful framework for human life.

The second point refers to the differences between tools and design techniques. We do not mean the actual tool kit we use as architects, but how we use it, and to what ends. The case of Gehry vs. Lévi-Strauss may shed some light on this subject. We all know the beautiful passages of *The Savage Mind* on the difference between the bricoleur and the scientist. The bricoleur works with no plan, with resources and procedures unlike normal technology. He works with ready-made rather than raw materials: products, fragments, leftovers, and bits and pieces; in the words of Lévi-Strauss, "a cultural sub-set" whose instrumentality he invents himself. The engineer distances himself from the here and now of the bricoleur and questions the "here and now and beyond" (the universe in the words of Lévi-Strauss) knowledge on the basis of the nature/culture relationship of his time, and selects the material resources that are best suited to constructing given the

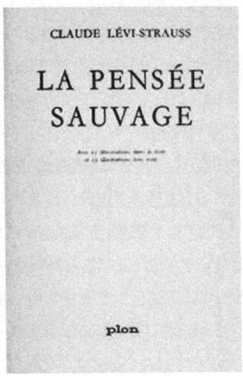

Claude Lévi-Strauss, *The Savage Mind*, 1962

objective he has in mind. These are two completely different worlds which underpin two different types of material culture. Seemingly, in an initial reading, to speak of design techniques is to speak of the means, to consider that the differences between them—such as representation techniques ranging from hand-drawing to conical perspective and the use of parametric algorithms—have implications for the decision-making process in terms of what we feel is of interest to us to undertake as a project and why.

However, Frank Gehry—like many other architects in periods of technological transition—enables us to question assumptions that were made too hastily. He was an acclaimed bricoleur in his early career, a brilliant builder of houses made literally from the materials at hand and assembled with the immediacy typical of the bricoleur. Few

Frank Gehry's residence in Santa Monica (top) and Walt Disney Concert Hall in Los Angeles

will doubt this methodological beginning, yet the fact remains that today with Gehry Technologies and the use of CATIA and other advanced computer-assisted design programs, Gehry's office pioneers an algorithmic research system which is at the forefront of the profession. However, it is significant that none of his ideas about what and how he wants his designs to be can be said to have undergone the slightest change (Mark Wigley saw him as a flag-bearer for Deconstructivism, despite the fact that he had not read Deconstructivist theory, and was certainly not influenced by it). In Gehry's work, there is a unique creative mind that imposes its will, based on the private act of deciding what and how things should be, over any scientific, cultural, or methodological contingency. Lévi-Strauss solves this apparent contradiction with his duality between the bricoleur and the scientist in an evasively vague paragraph: "The problem of art has been touched on several times in the foregoing discussion, and it is worth showing briefly how, from this point of view, art lies half-way between scientific knowledge and mythical or magical thought. It is common knowledge that the artist is both something of a scientist and

Raymond Roussel, *Comment j'ai écrit certains de mes livres*, 1935

of a 'bricoleur.' By his craftsmanship he constructs a material object which is also an object of knowledge." Many have wondered about creative processes and their extraordinary positioning in a corner of psychologically obscure subjectivity which contends with petty practical matters and giant abstractions. The everyday routines of professional practice are met by great theories on paradigm shifts whose resources answer to none of these conditions. Constraints and instinctive gestures, far removed from any subjugation, of which we are never fully aware act like secret agents of architecture as artistic practice.

Frequently, these gestures are based on issues so far removed from those objectively involved in the project that merely to mention them would be to greatly endanger the designer's credibility. For this reason, they are the most profound manifestation of the artistic nature of architecture compared to creation in science or engineering, for instance. This artistic condition is calibrated in terms of how often the design techniques actually employed by us architects are removed from any functionality—in no way responding to the question posed, nor being based on any objective data provided to the architect. On the other hand, they have a significant dose of whimsical, perverse, and childish play about them—not by going against the grain, but more by avoiding the expected.

They show that only the new or unexpected could wring out the artistic condition; the "as I desired" with which Cervantes proudly ends *Don Quixote*—the shortest design technique manifesto ever written. The great text by Raymond Roussel, *How I Wrote Certain of My Books*, including such works as *Locus Solus* and others, is an essential reference, a title which could be transferred directly to this symposium—"How I designed certain of my projects"—and which emphasizes willingly imposed and utterly irrational constraints on the work, such as enforcing certain symmetries on the first and the final words, almost turning his works into a giant palindrome by setting out the words of the start and the ending in a highly random fashion, along with many other evidently arbitrary techniques. However, beyond its specific, playful, and Dadaist randomness, this is a book written by a writer on creation, and as such he speaks to us in an extremely surprising language in which nothing is as might be thought from outside the creative moment. By performing a coldly descriptive, quasi-forensic exercise on what seem to be extremely useless, unimaginable techniques, Raymond Roussel made an extraordinary contribution, which has helped many to understand—and continues to do so—that we are not alone in our quasi-obscure practices. The arbitrary, the obsessive, the meticulous, or the particular found in the private play on a word is not so much a decision as a necessity that furthermore, paradoxically, is not necessarily at odds with functionality, efficiency, and economy—common demands in our profession—and in fact is often surprisingly useful for such ends. These reflections, despite their embryonic state, are what drove us to swiftly write the summary that heads this symposium on design techniques: "At a moment of dissolution in design, technique is all an architect can grasp. Techniques occupy a beautifully indeterminate void on the fault line between theory and practice. Spared of reductive allegiance to either, design techniques are uniquely powerful. A technique may disrupt, innovate, communicate, or surprise. At the same time, techniques stand as silent markers of memberships—opaque envelopes delimiting communities of colleagues. Techniques are how novelty manifests itself in architecture, expanding and advancing the inner core of our discipline."

The hypothetical success in advancing the discipline by describing what we really do as if we were attending a group session at Alcoholics Anonymous is not at all guaranteed. Yet it is helpful to visualize the complex blend of subjectivity and knowledge that is implicit in real design processes, and to expose the fallacies of two professional practices cloaked in procedural objectivity. I am referring to both the commercial architectural practices defined in the term "corporate architecture" and the dogmatic discourses based on machine-centric processes where the creator and their authority (seem to) fade away following an elaborate exercise in methodical hyperobjectivity. It is precisely by removing the element of play, by wiping away any negative or reactive impulses, or any vestiges of subjectivity or humor, that the complete fallacy of corporate architectural production as real architecture is exposed, for it is unable to create its own content. This is why it dresses itself up as being "in fashion," while attempting to steal that spirit without risking its own money.

The second funeral would be made up of those who are unable to accept the element of play, the profound arbitrariness which lends meaning to life and creation, and who will never be able to envisage the advent of a new artist, that elementary instinct which enables us to "sniff out" those who are moving forward, those who are striving and seeing further. This would be the funeral of the dogmatists, charmed by the logic of discourses, with their audience of acolytes—among whom there are always a few false dogmatists in need of an objectivist discourse in the early stages of their careers, like so many young, early-career radicals—for whom time has made radical alterations to their discourse. How can we not mention cases such as those of Le Corbusier or Aldo Rossi, whose attempts to write books

on their own design procedures (*L'espace indicible* by the former, *La città analoga* by the latter) were deliberately abandoned? As if expressing the instinctive obscurantism of the acoustic space or the pleasures of collage and memory in Rossi were too obscene and contradictory with their early functionalist and typological-morphological discourses.
Is this text a discourse against theoretical construction or against scientific and cultural knowledge in the discipline; that is, against the need to know and study our discipline? This is not its intention. This text aims to reposition design techniques between theory and praxis, as momentary impulses whose foundations are still unknown to us, a location between two classic moments, a turning or transit point which is strictly *neither theory nor praxis*. In *Homo Ludens: A Study of the Play-Element in Culture* (1938), Johan Huizinga described play as a function of human life beyond logical, biological, or aesthetic definitions; a voluntary,

Johan Huizinga, *Homo Ludens*, 1938

pleasant, and free act creating the fiction of momentary order and hence generating a pleasurable feeling of beauty based on the tension, balance, contrast, variation, and development of an innate sense of ornament:

> In culture we find play as a given magnitude existing before culture itself existed, accompanying it and pervading it from the earliest beginnings right up to the phase of civilization we are now living in. We find play present everywhere as a well-defined quality of action which is different from "ordinary" life. We can disregard the question of how far science has succeeded in reducing this quality to quantitative factors.

In our opinion it has not. At all events it is precisely this quality, itself so characteristic of the form of life we call "play," which matters.[3]

Similarly, the emphasis on this moment of implosion of the conscious and unconscious universes that is the creative act has close ties with the idea developed by Richard Rorty on the creative processes as changes in vocabulary and approach:

> […] revolutionary achievements in the arts, in the sciences, and in moral and political thought typically occur when somebody realizes that two or more of our vocabularies are interfering with each other, and proceeds to invent a new vocabulary to replace both.[4] […] The gradual trial-and-error creation of a new, third, vocabulary—the sort of vocabulary developed by people like Galileo, Hegel, or the later Yeats—is not a discovery about how old vocabularies fit together. That is why it cannot be reached by an inferential process—by starting with premises formulated in the old vocabularies. Such creations are not the result of successfully fitting together pieces of a puzzle. They are not discoveries of a reality behind the appearances, of an undistorted view of the whole picture with which to replace myopic views of its parts. The proper analogy is with the invention of new tools to take the place of old tools. To come up with such a vocabulary is more like discarding the lever and the chock because one has envisaged the pulley, or like discarding gesso and tempera because one has now figured out how to size canvas properly. […] The method is to redescribe lots and lots of things in new ways, until you have created a pattern of linguistic behavior which will tempt the rising generation to adopt it, thereby causing them to look for appropriate new forms of nonlinguistic behavior, for example, the adoption of new scientific equipment or new social institutions. This sort of philosophy does not work piece by piece, analyzing concept after concept, or testing thesis after thesis. Rather, it works holistically and

3   Huizinga, J. (1955). *Homo Ludens: A study of the play-element in culture*. Beacon Press, 4.
4   Rorty, R. (1989). *Contingency, irony, and solidarity*. Cambridge University Press, 12.

pragmatically. It says things like "try thinking of it this way"—or more specifically, "try to ignore the apparently futile traditional questions by substituting the following new and possibly interesting questions." It does not pretend to have a better candidate for doing the same old things we did when we spoke in the old way. Rather, it suggests that we might want to stop doing those things and do something else. But it does not argue for this suggestion on the basis of antecedent criteria common to the old and the new language games.

For just insofar as the new language really is new, there will be no such criteria. Conforming to my own precepts, I am not going to offer arguments against the vocabulary I want to replace. Instead,

Richard Rorty, *Contingency, Irony, and Solidarity*, 1989

I am going to try to make the vocabulary I favor look attractive by showing how it may be used to describe a variety of topics.[5]

New vocabularies and new approaches rise above their precursors and impose themselves through the beauty and novelty emanating from them. They speak a new language which becomes our own. They are also products of an inspiration whose roots are unknown to us.

5   Rorty, R. (1989). *Contingency, irony, and solidarity*. Cambridge University Press, 9.

3. Dualisms[6]

Most historic architecture draws its composite tension from two theoretically incompatible morphological organizations that correspond to different disciplines or languages. This composite tension usually involves the union of two organizations that possess both a degree of compatibility and a degree of incompatibility, leading to the appearance of a kind of "Frankenstein's monster"—a hybrid, characterized by dualism. These types of unions between different forms and a degree of materials can be carried out physically—in which case the assemblage will probably display seams and scars—or by processes of chemical fusion, giving the "monster" the appearance of a unique organism whose greatest visual effect is a new, surprising "naturalness."

From a thermodynamic viewpoint, these tensions can be regarded as characteristic of the flow of heat between sources and sinks or between degrees of energetic passivity and activity, simultaneously combining lightness and mass, order and disorder, natural passive processes and thermal engines. The processes of construction can also be addressed by introducing this sort of duality; for instance, by handcrafting some areas and using robotized production in others.

Contemporary architects' attention to machines has not ventured as far as the physics or the spatial structure of thermal devices. A close look at different machines—such as the heat exchanger, the Stirling engine, and the cooling unit—allows us to understand not only the precise relationship between form, material, and flow, but also the dual nature of any thermal mechanism at any scale, including buildings. In short, though repellent and alien to the modern orthodoxy, these dualities are the motor of thermodynamic vitality at all scales and for any project.

Dualisms act not only performatively but also in a creative and composite way. They are at once constraints and formative opportunities. They can be influenced by objective conditions. But dualisms are also related to the strategic techniques of a design, used to create a catalyzing tension in plots devoid of qualities or attributes. Strategic dualism is amazingly efficient in contrasting program and context as the

[6] This text brings together materials from the Harvard GSD exhibition of the same name (2014) about the work of the architectural office Ábalos+Sentkiewicz (AS+) and from a conference and conversation hosted at Harvard GSD (February 25, 2015) in the context of the "Design Techniques" symposium.

exclusive determinants of form (which are employed in the design of almost all "corporate" offices).

From our viewpoint, centered on cultural, social, economic, and energetic performativity, it is interesting to see how these dualisms—which compose self-organizing feedback systems—can introduce a territory of everyone and no-one, providing solutions that tend to center more on paradoxes than on objectifiable rationality. Fantastic examples of this can be found well beyond the field of architecture, from Mary Shelley's *Frankenstein*, initially a competition among friends, to Raymond Roussel's *How I Wrote Certain of My Books*, a technique of self-imposed mechanisms, indifferent to the purpose of the project and its local conditions.

In our projects over the years, one thing that stands out is the consistent commitment to diverse, interdisciplinary approaches which incorporate material and geometric resources that often seem paradoxical. These approaches frequently combine the massive and the intricate; the technical use of natural elements with the ornamental, landscape use of technical materials.

It is now some years ago that we formulated a new "naturalness" in which the hybrid perspective of a thermodynamic approach to architecture acquired the value of an operating system, leading to the first of the projects presented in this exhibition: the hotel and convention center on the M-40 in Madrid:

> Sensitivity to nature-oriented policies has influenced technical paradigms, with interest shifting from high-tech experiments—a relic of the modern spirit—to hybrid models, where the accent is placed on the interaction between massive and energetically inert natural materials and highly sophisticated, lightweight, and energetically active artificial materials that respond sensitively to environmental variation, giving rise to composite systems in which the former are responsible for accumulating and reducing exchanges while the latter act as generators, harnessing energy resources.
>
> This new technological model implies a shift from aspects of material organization—mass

production, simplified assembly, time and cost optimization, and the like—to the rational organization of energy cycles during both production and upkeep of the building. This shift now enables us to design systems that are not guided by the coherence and unity of materials but by environmental coherence, thereby opening up the field to experimentation in which the coherent mix of heterogeneous materials is a new and characteristic visual feature. This hybrid materiality involves a thoroughgoing transformation of aesthetic ideals in keeping with the intermixing of our human landscapes. This hybrid technique or "*mestizo* aesthetic" opens the door to what we have called *dualisms*.[7]

Dualisms have a long history in philosophy. The term "dualism" was originally coined to denote "co-eternal binary oppositions." Its other definition is: "A system that contains two essential parts." This is the extent of the definitions provided by a cursory Google search. It refrains from articulating how these two co-eternal oppositions live together. Our interest is not to answer any kind of formal "synthesis," but to maintain the opposition of the poles, and to preserve the tension created by things that cannot merge into one and are destined to live together while being different.

Dualism—the idea that a project can be designed with two radically different systems, ideas, or forms—has an aesthetic effect that is unrelated to beauty or ugliness in any clear way, but can be described as bizarre, provocative, sometimes absurd, sometimes surprising, attractive, maybe different, or just curious. Intriguingly, all of these words have a genealogy in aesthetics rooted in the Picturesque. Also, provocative avant-garde works from the beginning of the twentieth century shared similar ideas of the absurd, the surprising, the different, or the bizarre.

Dualism is at odds with synthetic form—it is about a plurality of forms and materials living together. At the same time, dualism is about performance, which also contains the word "form." While Renata and I were designing our first project together—containing huge highly passive volumes floating

[7] "A New Naturalism (7 Micromanifestos)," in *2G 22: Ábalos&Herreros*. Barcelona: Editorial Gustavo Gili, 2002.

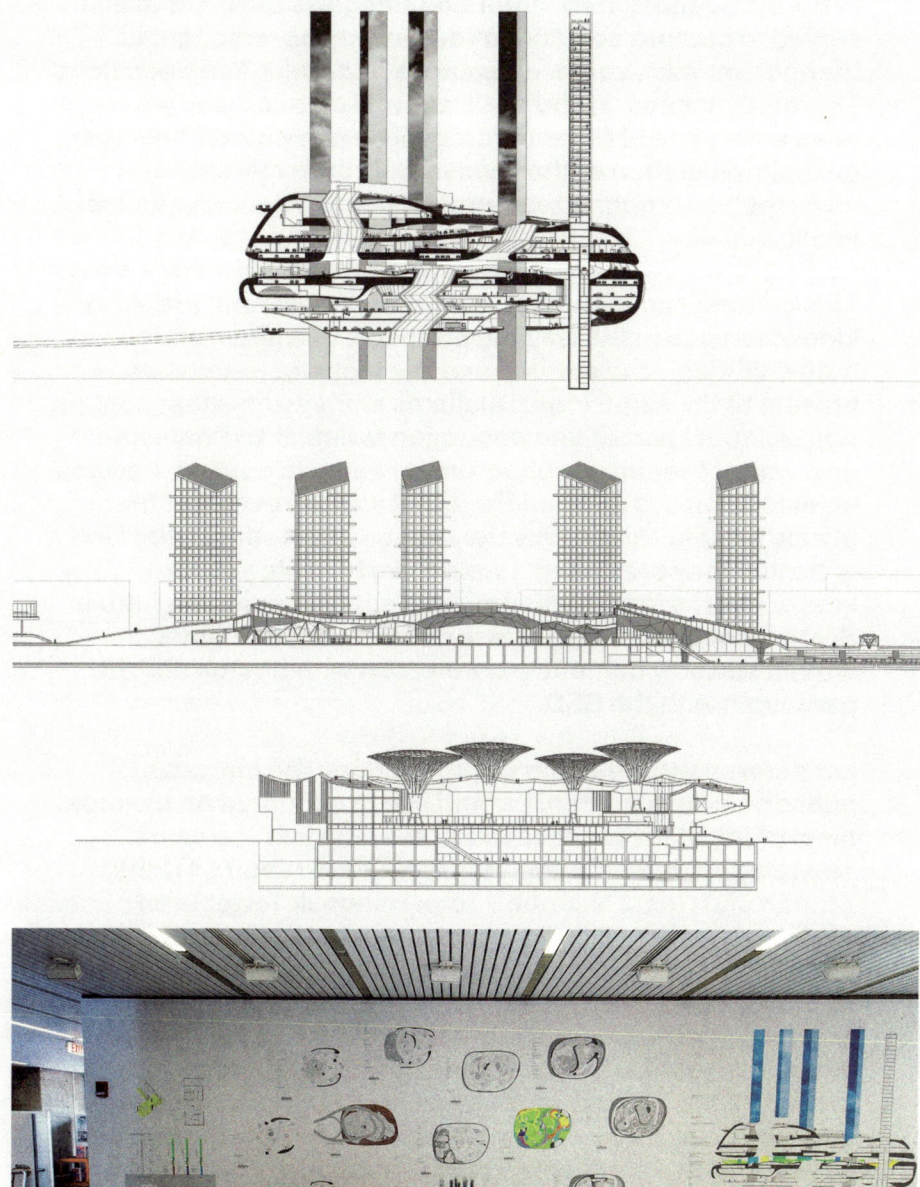

Ábalos+Sentkiewicz projects at Harvard GSD's exhibition *Dualisms*. (From top to bottom) M-40 mixed-use building in Madrid, 1997; Intermodal Station and urban plan in Logroño, 2006–2020; Zhuhai Contemporary Art Museum, 2014

in the air, supported by super-slender glass towers that also served to capture solar radiation—we discovered that in thermodynamics you need sources and sinks. You need flow. Thermodynamics is, above all, about dynamics, and you need difference in order to force these dynamics. If this is an over-simplification of thermodynamic principles, it nevertheless emphasizes a crucial point: thermodynamics implies duality.

This cultural and technical understanding of form creates a kind of tension in the way the project is designed, and both dualities—the cultural and the technical—must be present at the same time. Dualisms are "systems that contain two essential parts," and becoming aware of this reveals new ways of seeing architecture, of being in our own designs or historic places and buildings that we love even if at first glance we don't know why they are so interesting, what kind of beauty they are hiding. I would like to invite you on a kind of short trip through time and space, beginning here in Boston, but even if we move to other places and times, we will still stay somehow connected with Boston and, in particular, with the GSD.

Let's start now by visiting Copley Square, the important public square in Boston. I would like to comment on the most fascinating place we have found over the last few years. The relationship between Henry H. Richardson's Trinity Church and Henry N. Cobb's John Hancock Tower is an amazing one. We all know this dualism well, and know how closely these names are connected with this school. Obviously, there are many interpretations, but it is very clear that these two buildings form one of the most unbalanced and bizarre couples in the whole city. But even to those who are not experts in architecture, they look like a couple— a very odd one, but a couple nonetheless—or in our words, an active duality. This duality, created in time, is the result of a clear dialogue that is not based on trying to merge the two in any way. The Hancock is skewed to allow for a view of the church and the cloister as an ensemble from the street. There is another more interesting explanation. The first time I thought about what was so attractive about this relationship, I thought it was a kind of anthropomorphic relation rather than an architectural one. And I continue to see it as a young, gigantic NBA player standing to lead an old lady dressed in elegant traditional attire to sit down, or letting her enter the square first. I know this sounds like a joke, but I cannot describe it in other terms: it embodies the respectful attitude of a young man toward an old lady. At the same time, the relation of each building to nature is completely different. Richardson's is

Henry N. Cobb's John Hancock Tower, 1976, and Henry H. Richardson's Trinity Church, 1877, at Copley Square, Boston

completely rooted in the earth, it is absolutely material, it is almost part of the place, made of the same matter. Whereas Cobb's is dematerialized, almost floating. One is connected with the earth and the other is connected with the air.

Also at Copley Square, we all know and many admire the Boston Public Library (1895) by McKim, Mead & White. Some like it a lot. I think it is fine but boring, like a Durand drawing—almost industrial, dry, and graphic—even though it's made of nice granite. And it just stands there, proud of its immaculate figure, doing nothing in the middle of an amazing drama, a bizarre drama that means nothing to it. The dualism is also one between Europe and America, and this is important. As some of you might know, the Trinity Church is rooted in the Spanish Romanesque, which Richardson admired while studying in Paris and touring Spain, while the other is an American invention: the skyscraper. And this one, the John Hancock, is probably the last proper American skyscraper. Dematerialized, beautiful, a pure gesture: the John Hancock is a dialogue and duality that is permanent, and it expands from form to philosophy—in aesthetic terms as well as philosophically. One—Richardson's—is clearly connected with transcendentalism, while the other—Cobb's—is rooted in Minimalism, which at the time was becoming not just a form of vision but a form of thinking and living: a philosophy. All of these dualities create an interesting tension that is not just geometrical but also conceptual, material, and permeates every order, defining one of the most intense urban spaces in the US.

Another building in Boston (in Cambridge, in fact) is by another figure closely connected with this school (and with me for obvious reasons): Josep Lluís Sert. Let's visit the house he built a couple of blocks away from here—a really small and incredibly interesting house. It is really strange to use a patio or courtyard in the wintry climate that we have here. Thanks to Inés Zalduendo we had the chance to visit it in May, and as we were approaching, we began to perceive the characteristic scent of the wonderful Mediterranean pines. The smell shocked us: it was a smell at odds with the surrounding context, so before knocking on the door we discovered and admired the seven pines strategically planted around the house, which I guess no architects pay attention to, but we immediately understood that they were planted by Josep Lluís and his wife Moncha. The current owners of the house, who knew them quite well, confirmed this point. It might seem like a minor detail, but for someone who lives in the house and comes from the Mediterranean to live in Cambridge, it is not just an ornamental detail. The house is a patio house, and patio houses are made to create an interior outdoor space in addition to an exterior one. This duality is very efficient at amplifying the virtual scale of the house, relating it with the context, while the patio preserves the intimacy of its interior spaces. So it is important to notice that the pines are there to create a personal and evocative context, a context they loved. But the trees are not just there for their scent. They also create an exclusive image from the house: from the interior space, the surroundings are hidden; the windows reveal nothing but a strategic view of other pines. You see nothing but pines. But then, things get

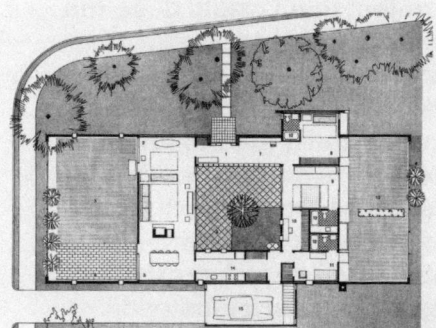

Josep Lluís Sert's house in Cambridge, 1957

more serious. First of all, the idea of coming to Boston to a house that is emotionally connected with Ibiza, where they had their summer house—likewise a patio house surrounded by pines—is as beautiful as it is crazy. They wanted to bring something to Cambridge that in thermodynamic terms was radically absurd, but in cultural terms was completely consistent. And frankly, I would love to be able to smell pines from our house in Cambridge too. At the same time, the idea of a house's trees becoming the center of a project is a dualistic idea, a beautiful idea that we learned and used almost literally some months later in our design for the Zhuhai museum. The patio was a key element of the project, and was directly connected with the building's hot and humid climate. And we designed artificial trees that combine form and performance to increase comfort in the outdoor space and provide character and a context to the whole design. They act differently to those at Sert's house. While they are clearly indebted to Sert's pines in the sense that they bring comfort and a pleasant experience, they also recharacterize the whole area.

We can move now to the present, to another GSD figure, Rem Koolhaas, and discuss the project that I would describe as marking the arrival of a new contemporary condition in architecture: the Paris Library. This is a project that moved us from Modernism and its concomitant epiphenomena to a genuinely different cultural position and understanding of the discipline. Probably, if it were to be built, as is often the case, it wouldn't be as magical as it is as a non-site, dualistic project. Nevertheless, it provides an image of the anti-skyscraper. It shifts the proportions and internalizes the excavation, placing the emphasis on the interior instead of the exterior. The modern skyscraper is distinguished by its slender profile and dominant, controlling vision. This is the complete opposite. It reverses the whole tradition of skyscrapers. Paradoxically, it is somehow a direct heir of Le Corbusier, because it can be seen as a kind of gigantic Villa Savoye. It literally quotes (or just plays with?) Le Corbusier—the promenade as an excavation, a rollercoaster that ends in a loop and balcony on the upper floor. But it creates an incredible tension between these excavated parts and the mass of information that forms the solid cube. The balcony is the relationship that is conveyed to the exterior. The façade is completely banal, intentionally uninteresting. It reminds me of another great Parisian architectural commentator, Jacques Tati, and his film *Playtime*, where you stand permanently in infinite interiors and only see Paris in the glass reflection of a revolving door. Here, you don't see Paris at all. Perhaps you recall that Koolhaas only shows an elevation drawing with a kind of cloud as the façade's curtain wall motif. All of these gestures and ideas constitute a collection of contradictions with the tradition of the skyscraper. And the relation with Le Corbusier is hilarious; it is based on creating very interesting paradoxes that comprise the building's intellectual dualism: while it pretends to be a skyscraper, it is a comment on Le Corbusier's organization of interior Picturesque architectural promenades. But they are now blandly gesturing in a massive, solid, and opaque cube.

When Peter Cook gave a lecture here some weeks ago, he mentioned Ludwig Leo in Berlin: another beautiful monster, the Circulation Tank at the Hydraulics Research Center in

Circulation Tank at the Hydraulics Research Center, Ludwig Leo. Berlin, 1974
Whitney Museum extension, OMA. New York, 2001

Berlin-Tiergarten, developed between 1967 and 1974. This is a real built monster; a beautiful pink dual monster. Technically, it has a relationship with the canal where it is located, but it has remained for many decades as one of the most interesting and attractive buildings in Berlin because of the brutality of its dual composition. There is a close figural relationship with another of Koolhaas's proposals, in this case for the Whitney Museum extension in New York City—another great OMA project, in my opinion. Again, there is a clear dualism—a tension and intensity between the original and the new Whitney, with the latter taking on the appearance of a veritable monster approaching Breuer's building, in order to definitively transform its role as a protagonist in the urban fabric. Some parts of the Ludwig Leo building as well as Koolhaas's Paris Library proposal are somehow present in this frustrated entry into the Whitney expansion competition. It's a real pity not to see it built.

To finish with some contemporary examples I have to take you to visit another work by other professors at this school: Jacques Herzog and Pierre de Meuron, who have recently finished a dualistic project, the Elbphilharmonie in Hamburg, probably one of the high points of their career. The ritual promenade on the escalators to the upper floors has some relationships to Rem Koolhaas's library. It is again a solid form excavated by a promenade, and a cavern instead of a rollercoaster, in this case parasitizing a preexisting industrial building, now playing the role of a podium. And the main hall can be seen as a grotto in the magma of its conventional slabs. This monstrous condition is shown in the stratification of its materiality, a timed kind of strata that emphasizes its relationship with the Elbe River.

We might continue by visiting an entire Picturesque collection of monstrous dualisms linked to the city and the GSD, but I would prefer to move on to other places and other times. For example, Diocletian's Palace in Spalato (Split). This amazing Roman palace facing the Adriatic Sea evolved from its original organization into a medieval village, reversing and reusing many of its monumental forms and materials. On a monumental scale, it exemplifies what we might consider a case of dualism in time, or "entropic dualism." It happens frequently and creates a kind of monumental differentiation, showing simultaneously a before and an after, a kind of construct of diverse cultures overlapping in an entropic ensemble. The combinations of the Roman order and the Gothic reuse of the ruins produces one of the most evocative and pleasant features of the Mediterranean coast. Nearly all of the elements that were important to the

Roman period have been recontextualized, changed in scale and use. What was a temple has now become a piazza, reversing the use of the space, changing the sacred into the

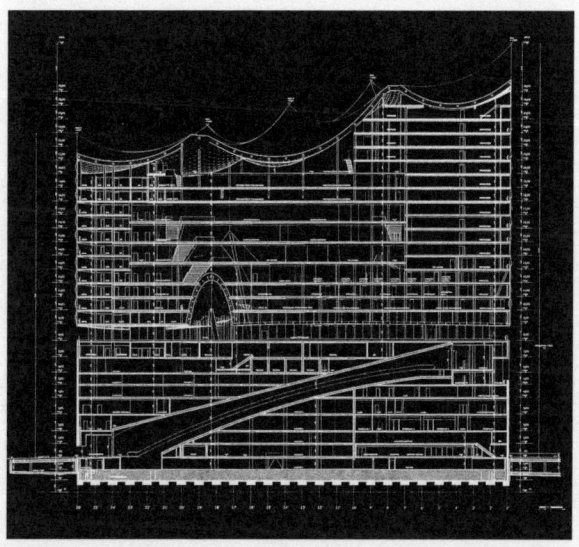

Elbphilharmonie, Herzog & de Meuron. Hamburg, 2001–2016

profane, the interior into the exterior, the private into the public, the emperor's palace into a medieval village. And the effect of the stratification of culture generates a unique and amazingly rich experience—an experience that Aldo Rossi

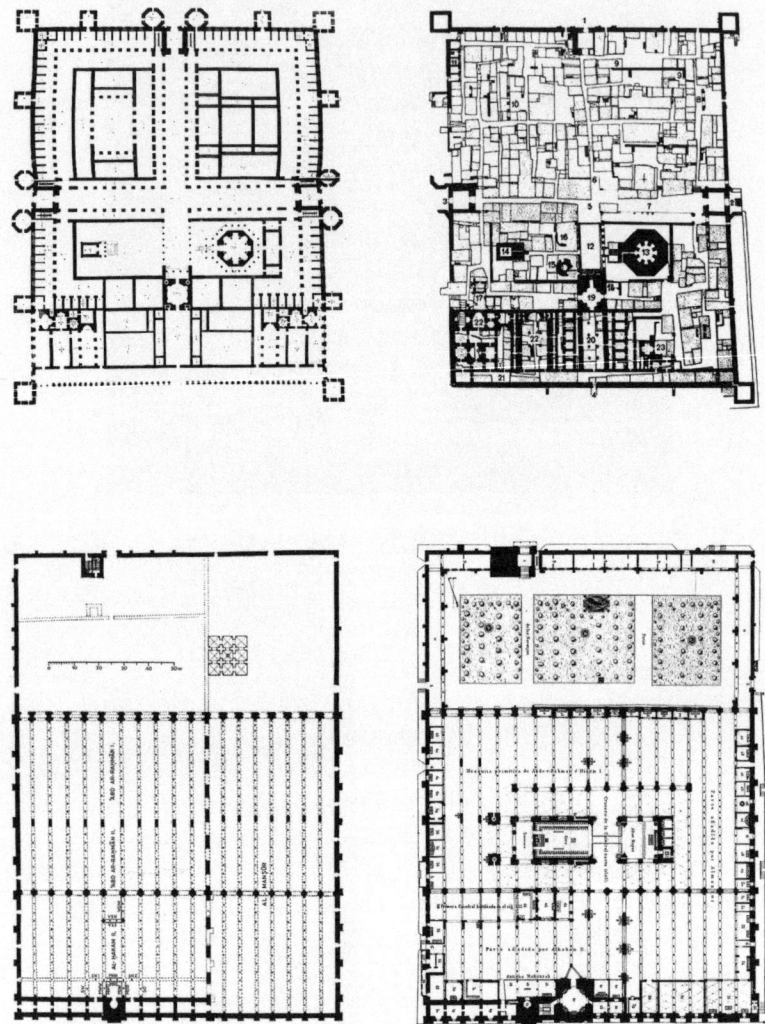

**Floor plan of Diocletian's Palace in Split, fourth century, and Gothic-era Split, Croatia, seventh to thirteenth centuries
Córdoba's mosque, original plan, eighth to tenth centuries, and the cathedral transformation plan, sixteenth century**

loved and discussed frequently as exemplifying the persistence of form in the city.

If we move to Córdoba, Spain, we find another terrific example, Jorge Silvetti's and Rafael Moneo's favorite: the Mezquita of Córdoba, built on the site and with the materials of the original Roman forum. So it has three strata: the Moorish construction of the mosque certainly had a lot of expansion phases throughout time and made great use of the rich marble columns of the Roman forum. But when the Christians took the city, they incorporated a cathedral into the forest of Roman columns that constituted the mosque, a cathedral that respects the rhythm of the mosque's overall composition and uses its internal walls as structural buttresses. It creates a unique type of cultural monster, but at the same time it becomes a wonderful expression of the adaptive capacity of the organizing scheme as well as the virtuosity of the cathedral's architect to manage the situation.

The two interior spaces (cathedral and mosque) are completely differentiated despite their careful geometric assimilation. The mosque's dark horizontality contrasts with the church's vertical brightness; Roman columns support Moorish arches that are embraced by late-Gothic and Renaissance structures. The minaret is likewise transformed into a campanile simply by changing the form and style of the upper part, an idea repeated in Seville's Giralda, which had a huge influence on the American art deco skyscrapers—another instance of time travel in the dialogue between Europe and America. All of these ingredients are successful temporal or entropic dualisms. The interior images of the mosque-cathedral that you can see on the internet are all artificially lit. When you switch off the lights—and this entails a three-hour wait and some tips to attendants—the interior reveals its incredible original beauty. It is very dark, your eyes need to adapt for some minutes. But once they have, the arches disappear into the darkness.

Then on one side, the Gothic-Renaissance hybrid cathedral introduces an explosion of vertical light. Once inside, you can see that both moments and styles, which are so difficult to combine, establish a pact and agree to coexist, maintaining their specificity and creating a very special harmony, mainly accommodated by the Roman columns. And so it is a synthesis of the Mediterranean cultures merging to form one specific dual or triple monster.

Another Spanish building in the same vein is the Monastery of El Escorial, a gigantic building that combined a cathedral with a monastery and a palace to mimic the monumental

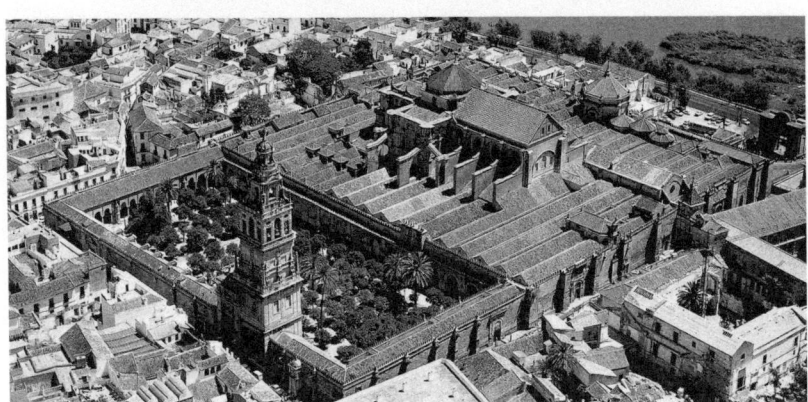

Interior and aerial view of the mosque-cathedral in Córdoba, Spain

scale and spatial organization of Diocletian's Palace. El Escorial and Diocletian's Palace are the same size, but the sections and programs included in El Escorial are a sophisticated combination of classic and medieval typologies, local technologies, and figurative references that include a bizarre pitched roof brought to Castile by the Austrian royal family as a sign of their identity. The pitched roof is totally at odds with the traditions and the climate of Madrid. The family of Philip II brought it to Spain, thus initiating a tradition and a style that went on to proliferate throughout the region. Again, as happens with Sert's pines, transfers of local identity come and go, producing complex layers that show that nothing is objective in architectural design, that dualisms and monstrosity occupy many different spaces and layers while they travel through time.

We can leave off our travels in search of different types of dualisms here and conclude this lecture by bringing together two architects—Le Corbusier and Rem Koolhaas—who somehow comprise a modern/postmodern dualism all of their own. I'd like to round off this discussion by taking a closer look at their dualistic manifestos.

Le Corbusier is the master of Modernist dualisms—something especially visible in his books and manifestos. His titles, for example, are telling: *A House—A Palace*. This title is itself a manifesto, one whose meaning you can grasp before reading even a single page. If an architect connects the simplest house, and the most refined palace, then an entire conception of architecture is resolved—the whole system exists. Not many pass this test, but all the great ones do. Another great example of a visual dualistic manifesto is in pages 134–135 of *Vers une architecture*. These two pages compose the strongest architectural manifesto ever made—you need nothing more to understand the basics of Modernism and its internal battlefields. The multiform tensions between history and the future, static and mobile, fragile and solid, technique and memory, and many other dualities are condensed here and stated succinctly and unforgettably.

Something similar happens if we conclude with a visit to Koolhaas's latest manifesto from his Venice Architecture Biennale and in particular his installation in it. This is, perhaps, the only image from the 14th Biennale, which he curated, that we would all remember. It marks a very pertinent question here: Where are we now after 100 years of Modernism? Are we in the minutely controlled, air-conditioned environment of junk space? Or are we reconnecting with other cultures where form, matter, and ornament shaped architecture? Perhaps we are unable to resolve this conflict or duality nowadays. But maybe this conflict is the dualism that secretly intersects all the attempts to reach a new contemporary notion of architecture.

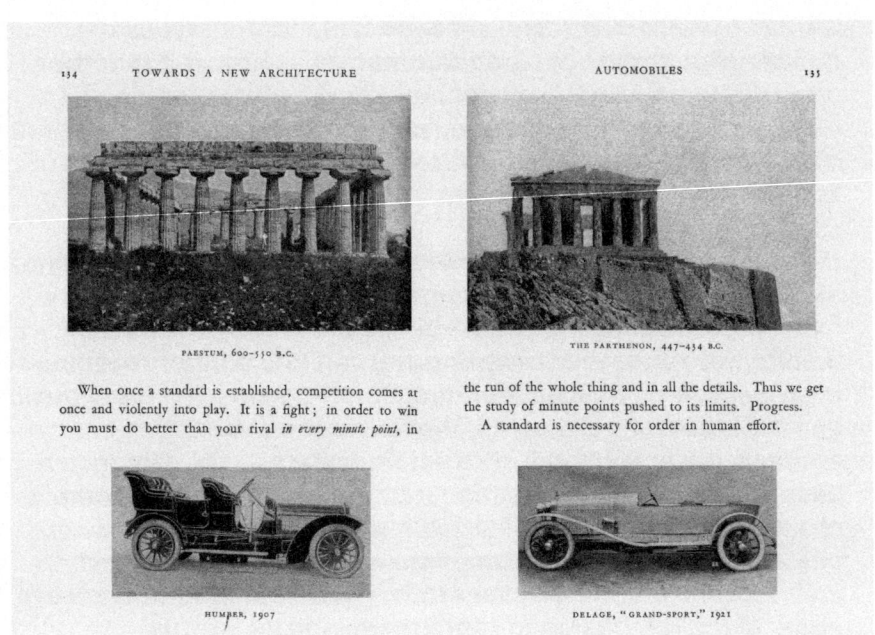

Pages 134–135 of Le Corbusier's book *Vers une architecture*, 1923

Bibliography:
Huizinga, J. (1938). *Homo ludens, proeve eener bepaling van het spel-element der cultuur*. English edition (1971). *Homo Ludens: A study of the play-element in culture*. Bacon Press.
Le Corbusier. (1923). *Vers une Architecture*. Éditions Crès.
Le Corbusier. (1928). *Une Maison—Un Palais*. Éditions Crès.
Lévi-Strauss, C. (1962). *La pensée sauvage*. English edition (1966). *The savage mind*. Weidenfeld & Nicolson.
Rorty, R. (1989). *Contingency, irony, and solidarity*. Cambridge University Press.
Roussel, R. (1935). *Comment j'ai écrit certains de mes livres*.

Ceiling, *Elements of Architecture*, Central Pavilion, 14th Venice Architecture Biennale, 2014

Photo Credits

Cover
© Estate of Robert Smithson. Image courtesy of James Cohan Gallery, New York

Somatic-Grotesque
© Fondation Le Corbusier, p. 15
© OMA, p. 17

Architecture for the Search for Knowledge
© Hans Kollhoff, p. 21
© OMA, pp. 27, 50
© Martin Hürlimann and others, pp. 32–33
© H Felton, p. 33
© Hisao Suzuki, pp. 36–37
© BIG, p. 50
© Herzog & de Meuron, p. 50
© Ábalos+Sentkiewicz, p. 50
© Caio Barboza, Sofia Blanco Santos, p. 53
© Huang Xiaokai, p. 53

A Conversation with Andrés de Vandelvira
© Fernando Chueca Goitia, Luis Cano Martínez, Ernesto Ontoria Guardamuros, Luis Berges Roldán, Ángel Nieto Donaire, Fotografía Baras (Úbeda), Fotografía Ortega (Jaén), pp. 61–86
© Museo Nacional del Prado, p. 90

A Monstrous Encounter Between Transcendentalism and Positivism
© National Park Service, Frederick Law Olmsted National Historic Site, Brookline, p. 93
© George Colbert and Guenter Vollath. Published by Greensward Foundation. Friends of Central Park, p. 94
© Museum of Fine Arts, Boston. Donation of Robert Jordan from the Eben D. Jordan Collection, p. 99
© The British Museum, London, p. 99
© Lee Friedlander, p. 118
© Fondation Le Corbusier, pp. 119, 125, 128
© The Olmsted Archives, Frederick Law Olmsted National Historic Site, Brookline, pp. 125, 128

Robert Smithson: The Picturesque Entropologist
© Nancy Holt. Estate of Robert Smithson. Images courtesy of James Cohan Gallery, New York, p. 133
© Estate of Robert Smithson. Images courtesy of James Cohan Gallery, New York, pp. 135–153

© Estate of Robert Smithson. Photograph by Gianfranco Gorgoni. Image courtesy of James Cohan Gallery, New York, p. 148
© The Museum of Modern Art, New York. Donation of Howard Gilman Foundation, p. 141

Three Delirious Skyscrapers
© The Museum of Modern Art, New York, p. 160
© Christiane Schily, Susanne Kiefer-Taut, Le Thanh Thuy Taut, Emmy Lorenz/Akademie der Künste, Berlin, Bruno-Taut-Archiv, pp. 157–169
© Ábalos+Sentkiewicz, pp. 171, 185–188
© José Hevia, p. 171

Dualisms
© Tim Street Porter, p. 197
© Lara Swimmer, p. 197
© Justin Knight, p. 207
© Philipp Lohöfener/Wüstenrot Stiftung, p. 215
© OMA, p. 212
© Herzog & de Meuron, p. 212
© Fondation Le Corbusier, p. 220
© Francesco Galli, p. 221

Absolute Beginners

Collaborators: Sofía Blanco Santos, José de Andrés Moncayo
Translation: Gegensatz Translation Collective, Joel Scott
Proofreading: Dean Drake
Graphic design: Samuel Bänziger, Rosario Florio, and Larissa Kasper
Image processing: Marjeta Morinc
Printing and binding: DZA Druckerei zu Altenburg GmbH, Thuringia, Germany
Typeface: Neue Haas Unica Pro

© 2022 Iñaki Ábalos and Park Books AG, Zurich
© for the images: see photo credits
© for the text: the author

Park Books
Niederdorfstrasse 54
8001 Zurich
Switzerland

www.park-books.com

Park Books is being supported by the Federal Office of Culture with a general subsidy for the years 2021–2024.

All rights reserved; no part of this publication may be reproduced, stored in a retrieval system, or transmitted in any form or by any means, electronic, mechanical, photocopying, recording, or otherwise, without the prior written consent of the publisher.

ISBN 978-3-03860-287-3